Dreaming Myself into Old Age

Dreaming Myself into Old Age

One Woman's Search for Meaning

Lily Iona MacKenzie

SHANTI ARTS PUBLISHING
BRUNSWICK, MAINE

Dreaming Myself into Old Age:
One Woman's Search for Meaning

Copyright © 2023 Lily Iona MacKenzie

Published by Shanti Arts Publishing

Cover and interior design by Shanti Arts Designs
Interior artwork by Lily Iona MacKenzie and used with her permission
Cover image by Quang Nguyen Vinh on pexels.com

"They Did Not Make Conversation," copyright © 1984 by Kathleen Fraser; from SOMETHING (EVEN HUMAN VOICES) IN THE FOREGROUND, A LAKE. Used by permission of Kelsey Street Press. All rights reserved.

"Pythagorean Silence: I, Pearl Harbor," by Susan Howe, from EUROPE OF TRUSTS, copyright ©1990 by Susan Howe. Reprinted by permission of New Directions Publishing Corp.

"The Magician's Retreat," copyright © 1981 by Clive E. Driver, Literary Executor of the Estate of Marianne Moore; from THE COMPLETE POEMS OF MARIANNE MOORE by Marianne Moore. Used by permission of Viking Books, an imprint of Penguin Publishing Group, a division of Penguin Random House LLC. All rights reserved.

"The Moon Maiden," by Lily Iona MacKenzie, first appeared in THE SAN FRANCISCO JUNG JOURNAL, September, 2022.

"Mundus Imaginalis: Reflections After Seeing Magritte," by Lily Iona MacKenzie, first appeared in THE SAN FRANCISCO JUNG JOURNAL, November, 2002.

"The Cheval Glass," copyright © 1995 by Andrew Joron and Andrew Zawacki, Literary Co-executors of the Estate of Gustaf Sobin; from BY THE BIAS OF SOUND: SELECTED POEMS: 1974–1994 by Gustaf Sobin. Used by permission of the forementioned estate. All rights reserved.

"Work in Progress: Dusk" from New Math by Cole Swensen. Copyright ©1988 by Cole Swensen. Used by permission of HarperCollins Publishers.

Scriptures taken from the Holy Bible, New International Version®, NIV®. Copyright © 1973, 1978, 1984, 2011 by Biblica, Inc.™ Used by permission of Zondervan. All rights reserved worldwide. www.zondervan.com The "NIV" and "New International Version" are trademarks registered in the United States Patent and Trademark Office by Biblica, Inc.™

Shanti Arts LLC
Brunswick, Maine
www.shantiarts.com

Printed in the United States of America

This book is a memoir, written from the author's recollections of experiences that occurred over many years. The dialogue presented in this book is not intended to represent word-for-word transcripts; events and scenes are not precise representations. The names and characteristics of some individuals have been changed to protect privacy. In all cases, the author has remained true to the feeling and meaning of what happened and what was said.

ISBN: 978-1-956056-91-4 (print; softcover)
ISBN: 978-1-956056-92-1 (ebook)

Library of Congress Control Number: 2023943671

I dedicate this book to all those I mention in the Acknowledgments, as well as others who have inspired me over the years to know myself: teachers, students, family members, friends, and more.

Thanks also to M's constant love and support.

Aging people should know that their lives are not mounting and unfolding but that an inexorable inner process forces the contraction of life. For a young person it is almost a sin—and certainly a danger—to be too much occupied with himself; but for the aging person it is a duty and a necessity to give serious attention to himself.

—Carl Jung

Let no one be slow to seek wisdom when he is young nor weary in search thereof when he is grown old. For no age is too early or too late for the health of the soul.

—Epicurus, "Letter to Menoeceus"

Old age is the most unexpected of all things that happen to a man.

—Leo Tolstoy

The meaning of life is death.

—Franz Kafka

The body gets old but the creative mechanism is refreshed, smoothed and oiled and honed.

—Maurice Sendak

CONTENTS

ACKNOWLEDGMENTS

IT TAKES A VILLAGE FOR MANY THINGS TO TRANSPIRE, AND it's certainly true of this book. A poet and novel writer until now, I didn't start out to publish a hybrid memoir. The idea arose partly because I teach the art of memoir but also because dreaming has been such a huge part of my life since I started paying close attention to these nightly visitors in my twenties.

Recently, I've had the good fortune of reading early journals I kept, starting in the '70s. Dreams take up a large portion of the narrative that I carefully recorded in script, and they are as fascinating for me to read and try to decipher now as they were then. But that's a subject for another book (I hope!).

Clearly, dreams started me down a road that has taken me into byways that I otherwise may have missed. And along those paths I've encountered many people who have become close friends and mentors. Without them, I wouldn't be who I am today. Many I've mentioned in this narrative, especially M, my dear husband, who has been such an advocate for my writing and put up with many evenings when my writing segment for the day had to take precedent over spending time with him.

Family members, too, both from my origins (my sister and her husband, especially), and my wonderful son, who continues to inspire me, have given me strength and purpose. So, too, have the amazing extended family I entered when I married M. Too numerous to mention individually.

But ultimately, when it comes to publishing a book such as this, it takes a publisher's sensibilities to appreciate what I'm attempting. So I give a great shout of gratitude to Christine Cote, the imaginative and brave publisher of Shanti Arts Press. I fell in love with her productions years ago. When I finished writing *Dreaming Myself into Old Age*, her press was the one I hoped would publish it. Months ago now, she responded to my submission with the words "Wonderful book! I'd be thrilled to publish it." I was more than elated.

I'm also grateful to Solace Wales, author of *Braided in Fire: Black GIs and Tuscan Villagers on the Gothic Line* and Russell A. Lockhart, PhD, author of *The Final Interlude: Advancing Age and Life's End*, *Psyche Speaks*, and *Words as Eggs*. Both took considerable time out of their busy lives to read the manuscript and write blurbs for the cover.

I've already stated in the Epilogue how important Steve Joseph, MD, has been in my development, but I would be remiss not to acknowledge what an important presence he was and still is in my life. I'm forever grateful to the analytic relationship we developed over the years and the insights into myself and others that I derived from it. I hope the substance of this relationship comes through in these pages.

PROLOGUE

MAURICE SENDACK'S WORDS, "THE BODY GROWS OLD, BUT the creative mechanism gets oiled, polished, honed," make old age seem tolerable, almost desirable. From his perspective, our later years appear attractive, even preferable to youth if we take time for our creative abilities to develop fully, whether in the arts or some other endeavor. For some of us, it may happen when we're younger, though it's always a process in that we continually can expand and refine such skills. But for others similar to myself, a high school dropout at fifteen and a single mother just after turning seventeen, it can take longer.

Fifty-four years old when I married my current husband, M, an English professor and psychoanalyst, I'd just completed my second master's, this one in creative writing (the first had been in the humanities, and I had earned that degree at forty-five). I not only entered into what has become a long-lasting union with a man whom I love and respect deeply, but I also took on the task of helping him raise a four-year-old girl and a ten-year-old boy. At the same time, I was deepening my commitment to myself as a writer and part-time rhetoric teacher at the University of San Francisco (USF). All of this was certainly a creative endeavor, juggling late-in-life parenting (I'd already raised my own son, then an adult) with the challenges of establishing myself in this new family.

Now that I'm eighty-one, I can further test Sendack's ideas, especially since I've been developing this "creative mechanism" for many years as a writer of poetry, fiction, and non-fiction. Creativity also appears in my work as a teacher.

But I have a confession to make that I'm sure others can relate to. My internal age, the self that I'm writing from at this very moment, doesn't seem to recognize chronological time. Yes, I've put in eighty plus years on this earth, but my attitude and outlook are still youthful, something I've noticed in other older people who are fully invested in living. They manage to retain a zest for life in spite of many detriments, including ill health as well as other hurdles that can happen at any age.

It reminds me of how foolish I was as a young woman when I brashly claimed, "I want to live fast, love hard, and die young." I had no idea then what those words meant. It was the sixties, and it sounded cool to make such an outrageous statement. At that time, aging seemed to be a far-off country, and it didn't have great reviews. I didn't know what that life phase involved. Nor did I have a clue what my later years held in store for me, and, in many ways, I still don't, though when I see myself in the mirror while wearing my contact lenses, it's a shock. Without them, the lines in my face are less noticeable, but through the lenses, I see myself more clearly. Age lines are carving intriguing valleys into my skin, and I have no choice but to acknowledge that, yes, old age has caught up with me.

Still, I want to age gracefully, despite it sounding like vague, California new-agey talk. A way to remove all of the negative stuff from our later years. While the San Francisco Bay Area culture definitely has influenced me, I don't have a crystal collection, and I reserve judgment on unconventional ideas such as alternative medicine, auras, and energy fields. I confess, though, to periodically practicing both yoga and meditation, and I've done so since my early thirties. I believe these practices can deepen a relationship with our inner life. I'm also curious about astrology, the Tarot, and other Hermetic approaches, in spite of my strong skepticism.

I've hoped that gracefully will translate into thoughtfully and assume that if I do all of the right things—exercise regularly, meditate, eat healthy food, read extensively, keep learning new things, and enjoy good relationships—I might have an easier old age: not too many physical, mental, or emotional challenges. I also have thought that if I learn as much as I can about aging itself, if I understand the problems involved, I might deal with them in a more constructive way.

While doing the "right things" makes sense and living a balanced life could be valuable in the long run, it has given me the false belief that I can control my future—how my mind and body will react in my later years. This idea that we can overcome whatever comes our way has a heroic component. Our ego, the central organizing part of our conscious personality, tends to identify with the hero ideal, by which I mean the impulse to rescue, to lead, to succeed in the face of massive difficulties. These can be positive goals, but they also can mislead us into thinking we can conquer anything.

Now that I've entered old age, I realize how naive I've been. On a certain level, I didn't truly believe that one day I actually would face any obstacles, and in some ways, I still don't believe it. This assumption is something I constantly need to watch for. Having been blessed with good health for much of my life (though I've had structural problems that have needed surgical repair, such as a blocked kidney duct that had to be corrected and a partial knee replacement), it's difficult to imagine myself waking up and not feeling fully energetic, ready to meet the day's demands. I rarely take naps (though it was something I did frequently as a much younger woman) and can't picture myself lacking vigor, physically or mentally.

As I write these words, I have even more energy than when I was younger. I also, perhaps foolishly, assume it will continue. My reason? I have a role model that may be difficult to match. My mother lived to one hundred and one, and, until she turned ninety-five, she resided in a one-bedroom cottage, part of a senior complex in Calgary, and did her own shopping, laundry, meal preparation, and house cleaning. She was eligible for household help from the government, but Mum always scoured the place before the cleaner arrived, not wanting "to make the poor woman work too hard."

When she was ninety-two, Mum flew to San Francisco (where I live) from Calgary (where I grew up) to join me on her first trip to Mexico (Puerto Vallarta). She ran me ragged, up by 8 or 9 am, her hair set, dressed in a fashionable outfit (for hanging around the house, she wore stretch pants with a hip-length pullover top), face made up with rouge, mascara, eyebrow pencil, and bright red lipstick, ready to go. From the way she dressed, it was clear she still wanted men's attention, to be looked at admiringly as a sexual creature.

Each afternoon, eager for my own half-hour nap, I would ask her if she wanted to take one too. "No, I'm fine. You go ahead and lie down, dear. I'll just read or knit." And I had been concerned that traveling at her age would be too much for her! She seemed to have a bottomless reservoir of energy, enjoying the tours we took of ranchitas as well as boat cruises I'd organized, dancing with the waiters during these events.

Then at ninety-five, Mum learned she had colon cancer. The day before surgery was scheduled, she had her hair styled professionally. She also applied gobs of red polish to her fingernails so she'd look nice for her doctor and sang Scottish songs as orderlies wheeled her to the operating room. But even surgery couldn't keep her down for long.

I stayed with her throughout the whole process, except when she was in the actual surgery, and watched her insist on getting out of bed an hour after returning to her hospital room. She was not one to lollygag and never slept in, so being confined to the bed upset her. The nurses let her sit up for a while in a chair, concerned she'd do herself more damage by fighting against the restraints. The anesthetic still hadn't fully worn off and she was heavily sedated, but that moment was pure Mother in Action. She'd always exhibited an indomitable spirit, and even colon cancer surgery didn't keep her down for long.

That's when she left her cottage and moved into an assisted living facility, but she still fully engaged life head on, as interested in dressing up and attracting men, in having new adventures and experiences, as when she was a younger woman.

You can see why having this mother as a model makes it even more difficult for me to acknowledge that, first, I might not live as long as she did and, second, I may experience more physical problems. Just because she had such a blessed old age doesn't mean I will, even though I ride a stationary bike for two hundred and ten minutes a week and do full body workouts, including weights, three days a week. I also am careful about the food I prepare for our meals, mainly serving my husband and myself a Mediterranean diet, accompanied by wine.

In contrast, Mum never held back on anything edible that would give her pleasure. Ice cream. French fries. Meat and gravy. Candies and chocolates by the bushel. In the politically correct environment of Northern California, how can I compete with her? I down my probiotics and array of multivitamins, hoping they'll help me avoid the grim reaper, but I know how futile that is.

My awareness of life's unpredictability grew when my husband was diagnosed early in 2016 with bladder cancer. Throughout his life, my super healthy husband had never missed teaching a class or meeting with a patient because of illness. He seemed impermeable! He wasn't. So far, the cancer has remained localized in his bladder, and he has been in remission since being treated with radiation and chemotherapy. We're hoping he'll be one of the 90 percent who won't need further action. If he's part of the other 10 percent, he'll have to follow plan B, the removal of his bladder and prostate. It's a gamble, as his disease always is, but we have no choice.

Before cancer shook up our lives, we both had been able to push away the thought of death. Now it holds a central place. We no longer can buffer ourselves with the fallacy that if we don't think of the grim reaper's visit, we can keep him at bay. Instead of the endgame being something we'll face in the far distant future, it's fully present. No one gets out of this life alive! As reminders, we have two Mexican Catrina statues—female skeletons wearing glamorous floor-length dresses and huge, wide-brimmed floppy hats—posed on our living room mantel. The mirror behind them gives us four Catrinas in all, a cue to celebrate life but to remember we all must leave it one day.

The news that cancer was threatening my beloved partner came as a shock to me and was a wakeup call. In Carl Jung's jargon, the puella archetype, the eternal girl, has an active part in my personality, as it did with my mother. Yes, I've done a lot of growing over the years, and this eternal youth profile has modified greatly, but she is still a presence and views herself as forever young. Now this eternal girl is struggling to absorb that eventually she will lose her youthfulness, even though she still will be driven to explore new things and fly high, at least symbolically, whenever possible.

So, on the one hand, my husband's illness has grounded me more. But on the other hand, I haven't totally lost my tendency to act as if I will live forever. On a certain level, I believe I will. I don't think our lives necessarily end when we leave this earthly abode. But I haven't a clue what could be next or how it might manifest as I find organized religions' explanations simplistic. I'm assuming that just as traveling to a foreign country is usually completely different from our expectations, life after death will also defy our portrayals of it.

Meanwhile, I function as if I will live forever. While this attitude could be viewed as the eternal youth's way of totally denying death, of caving to American culture's embrace of youth, I believe it is one key to a successful old age. I want to approach each day with the same fervor as ever and to continue developing in all ways possible, keeping in mind the new limitations I'm facing. We don't need to believe in an afterlife in order to live as if this earthly one will never end.

DESCENT

ONE

A T THE BEGINNING OF 2012, IN MY SEVENTY-SECOND YEAR, I decided to return to analysis. I felt it was time to explore my fears of aging and dying. Fortunately, I found Dr. Y, a Jungian analyst who takes Medicare, freeing me to explore my new terrain—old age—without depleting our savings. He also is a psychiatrist, so he merges the rational world of science with the more mystical one Carl Jung embodies. Of course, Jung also was an MD, grounded in the scientific method. But for me, his esoteric ideas about the psyche, which I gorged on from the time I first discovered his writing in my late twenties, overshadowed the scientist. I love how he evokes the multiplicity of things—the magic, the mystery, the many levels to reality. The mythic dimension.

Dreams inhabit the mythic element. I see them as communications from a part of myself that knows more about me than my conscious ego does. In *Modern Man in Search of a Soul*, Jung says that "dreams may contain ineluctable truths, philosophical pronouncements, illusions, wild fantasies, memories, plans, anticipations, irrational experiences, even telepathic visions, and heaven knows what besides."

They also appear connected to magical realism. As a poet and fiction writer, magical realism travels naturally from my brain onto the page, allowing me to blend these different elements, the real and the surreal, each having an important role. But at the time I started this late-life analysis, I felt somewhat alienated from the mythic worldview, one consequence of living in modern times in a culture where the rational scientific stance dominates. I needed someone who could help me return to my core self.

Also, my husband is a classical Freudian analyst who doesn't share my Jungian perspective. I'm sure our relationship has contributed to me distancing myself at times from the more fabulous realm. So, while we both believe there is an unconscious, we have differing ideas about its breadth and depth, as well as how to access it. Since I value his tremendous intellect (among many other things, including his sweet heart!), I can see where I might feel overpowered at times by his different stance. Still, we share multiple other interests, including similar values and a passion for all of the arts. In Jungian parlance, we would be considered opposite psychological types.

Another major difference between us? I believe our everyday reality contains more than what our limited consciousness can apprehend. Knowing there is a supernatural level adds a richer quality to my everyday routine, one reason why magical realism is such a strong factor in my fiction. I don't deny realism. In fact, I love it. But I also love it when strange things disrupt the quotidian, as happens in my novel *Curva Peligrosa* (and other narratives I've written). Magical events envelope Curva, the main character, wherever she goes. Her twin brother materializes after being dead for twenty years. Ancient bones speak and come to life. A geyser bursts spontaneously from the earth on her Canadian farm, gushing water even during frigid winters.

I'm sure that much of what I do with dreams and in Jungian analysis appears mysterious to my husband. He jokingly accuses me of conducting secret rites in our study after he goes to sleep—lighting candles, doing "witchy" things.

Strange.

Mystifying.

For me, the study in our home acts as a conduit to my deeper self. My laptop—where I record my dreams, store my journals, and write—is parked there when I'm not using it elsewhere in the house. My portion of our study also has an art table equipped with watercolors, oil pastels, colored pencils, and other materials, ready to collect colors and shapes from the unconscious that choose to surface in that way.

All of this feeds into my interest in esoteric knowledge that has intensified as I age. I continue to deepen my understanding of what might await us after death, assuming the mystics and other religious seekers have made discoveries I can learn from. But I also wonder what might be happening around us that our limited vision prevents us from seeing. It's the same urge that attracted me to Jung's ideas in my late twenties.

I remember going to Tahoe on a camping trip with R, my

husband at that time, my young son from an earlier brief marriage, and another couple we were friends with as well as their three kids. In the evening, while the others sat around a campfire, drinking and chatting and laughing, I stole away to our tent and read Jung's *Man and His Symbols* by flashlight.

The world I fell into then thoroughly engrossed me, especially where Jung talks about the importance of dreams and how symbols convey knowledge that often can't be accessed in our usual discursive way of thinking. Symbols play a major role not only in dreams but also in transmitting material that enlarges our understanding of ourselves and of the world. As Jung points out, "A word or an image is symbolic when it implies something more than its obvious and immediate meaning." For example, we often apply feelings to various colors that take on a symbolic quality: black representing death; white standing for life and purity; red suggesting blood, passion, danger, and even immoral character. Symbolic images present one literal moment in time, but deeper layers of meaning lurk behind them. Francois Millet's 1857 painting *The Gleaners* features three black women in a field bent over while collecting leftovers from a harvest. While on the surface this painting is about three women gathering the harvest, it can be viewed in multiple ways, one of them being that it symbolizes the rural poor and their marginalization.

In reading about symbols in *Man and His Symbols*, I was reminded of my first exposure to them and what a powerful moment it was for me. In tenth grade, we read and discussed Edgar Alan Poe's poem "The Raven." When our teacher told us that the raven symbolized mournful and never-ending remembrance of the narrator's loss of his beloved Lenore, my ears perked up. It was my first (or the earliest I remember) encounter with the notion that language or images can have hidden meanings, that not everything is spelled out for us. On the denotative level, a raven, a common bird, flies into the narrator's house, but on the connotative one, the raven is much more than what it appears to be. It was an exciting moment for me, and I recall how often my hand shot up in later classes when I recognized symbols in the works we were reading.

Jung's comments in *Man and His Symbols* had a similar effect on me. After reading the book, I was seeing multiple meanings in almost everything around me, from baseball games I attended when my son was pitching to wandering through a mall. These pages introduced me to the unconscious, to the idea that behind everyday reality there are other layers to investigate. And, of course, it was behind my impetus to have eventually claimed my writer self. Having majored in English, I became adept at tracking down hidden meanings in the texts I explicated.

Jung's comments about dreams also had a strong impact on me. I was fascinated by his idea that dreams are a way the forgotten or unacknowledged aspects of our consciousness reach our awareness. He says, "It was the study of dreams that first enabled psychologists to investigate the unconscious aspect of conscious psychic events." A prolific dreamer, I was eager to know what I could learn from them.

From then on, I was hooked. Like Alice in Wonderland, I'd fallen down the rabbit hole and would be forever changed from this encounter. I learned that individuals not only have the personality they present to the outer world, but that they also have other personalities loitering beneath consciousness. As Jung points out, it isn't just the neurotic whose right hand doesn't know what the left hand is doing. It's a problem for most modern men and women.

At the time, I'd recently gone through an intense inner journey during a deep depression that had lasted a year, a period when I became interested in religion and also entered therapy for the first time with the Reverend Elmer Laursen, chaplain at San Francisco's UCSF Medical Center. He oversaw the counseling program there. The pastor at the Marin church where I'd recently been baptized referred me to Laursen. In addition to helping me find my way through this dark stage, Laursen also sparked my interest in psychology and spirituality, lending me books by Tillich (*The Courage to Be*), Buber (*I and Thou*), and material by other major thinkers, including *Dreams: God's Forgotten Language* by Jungian psychologist and Episcopal priest John Sanford. Along with Jung's writings, as well as work by other Jungians, Sanford's text gave me a foundation for my lifelong interest in dreams and their possible connection at times to the divine.

No wonder I became interested in Jung's psychology. It not only led me into the complexities of our individual selves, but it also made a link between our smaller-"s" self and the larger-"s" Self he believed shapes our psyches—the fulcrum of our beings. According to Frith Luton, a Zurich-trained Jungian analyst and psychotherapist, "Experiences of the self possess a numinosity characteristic of religious revelations. Hence, Jung believed there was no essential difference between the self as an experiential, psychological reality, and the traditional concept of a supreme deity."[1]

All this reminded me of the John Freeman interview with Jung filmed in 1959 when he was eighty-four. On the BBC program *Face to Face*, Jung told Freeman he'd grown up as a pastor's son in the Swiss Reformed Church, going to Sunday services and believing in God. Freeman asked whether Jung still believed in God. He answered, "Now? Difficult to answer. I know. I needn't, I don't need to believe. I know."

At a time when I had just begun my quest for a deeper understanding of myself and the universe, having an eminence like Jung make such a bold statement was astonishing and inspiring, an event that has stayed with me all these years. I was far from arriving at Jung's destination of "I know." But I wanted to have experiences that would give me similar confidence in something beyond my five senses. I also wanted to understand more about this divinity's existence. Therefore, it was comforting to discover someone like Jung whose faith was so powerful. A novice, I didn't know anything. I just hoped I might one day share Jung's belief in something beyond the visible world and find the same supreme confidence that he expressed.

Dreams strengthened my views that, as Hamlet says to Horatio, "There are more things in heaven and earth than are dreamt of in your philosophy." I wasn't expecting dreams to give irrefutable knowledge that God exists (though I wouldn't mind if that happened!). But they show how complex our inner lives are and how eagerly the unconscious wants to interact with the conscious ego. I continue to find this dynamic astounding, that there is a different consciousness than my waking smaller-"s" self. And dreams have increased my awareness of realms beyond my conscious understanding. This perspective has played itself out over and over in my life.

Since my late twenties, then, dreams have performed a major role. They remind me of funhouse mirrors that reflect back multiple images of ourselves, capturing how multifaceted we are. It's as if we have this inner being who knows us intimately and, through dream images and stories, broadens and deepens our self-understanding.

I'm constantly amazed at the ways in which this occurs. Recently, I dreamed I was riding in a car with M, who was driving. Upset because he kept his head turned to the left, absorbed by something he was seeing in that direction rather than on the road, I, of course, told him he needed to keep his eyes on the road at all times. I'd learned that most accidents occur in those seconds when we aren't paying attention. In this particular dream, I was taking an approach to driving that I'd learned from the conventional external world where my stance probably would have been the correct one.

But such rules don't necessarily exist in the unconscious, the inner realm. A different world, it often challenges our external perspective. Our laws and morals can be too restrictive for much of what happens outside of our awareness. So, I stepped back and asked myself what would happen if my ego self in the dream, who is criticizing my husband's driving, looked at the scene differently? Instead of being upset because he is staring at something to the left, I could loosen my "rules" and discover what has captured his attention. What am I missing because of my rigid attitude?

I realized that while the dream seemed to be speaking of a dynamic in the unconscious, it also could be offering me another way of thinking. How often in my conscious life do I use such directives to criticize my husband or shut him down rather than discover what knowledge and perspective he has that I don't have access to? We tend to mate with people who are opposite to us, and a long-term relationship gives us an opportunity to integrate certain qualities that our partner has that we don't.

Recent dreams have also shown images of me at different ages. I believe dreams can act as a kind of video camera, recording our various selves and rearranging them in these new narratives. Seeming to support this idea, recent dreams have contained videos of myself at different ages.

Each morning I capture in my journal as many dream fragments as I can remember. A therapist I worked with years ago referred to them as my New Testament, and I do feel the daily dialogue with them has a prayerful aspect in the sense that I'm communing with something deeper, something larger. I also believe that we don't have to consciously understand dreams to benefit from the potent imagery and symbols they convey. They affect us whether we "get them" or not, becoming part of our memory bank, energy deposits that we can draw from for a lifetime. So when I read Jungian analyst Russell Lockhart's view of dreams in a work he co-authored, *The Final Interlude*, I felt as if he was expressing an idea that was true for me as well. Lockhart says, "Where I feel truly and deeply at home is in the dream . . . I have stopped looking outside for home. I have found it inside. And the most inside is the dream. When I wake from a dream I have this feeling of having stepped out of my home." I thank him for naming this discovery for me and, I'm sure, for many others.

While organized religion has some answers and is important to many people, it doesn't satisfy my need for the esoteric. Dreams have become one of my replacements, adding multiple levels to what could be a bland existence. Giving my nightly wanderings in dreamscape the opportunity to penetrate daily life has made me more aware of another level to the psyche, that is, the human mind's totality, conscious and unconscious. And Jung is one of the few psychologists who has treated dreams seriously. Of course, Freud was his first teacher, but Jung didn't approach dreams as Freud did. Also, as something of a mystic, Jung was open to exploring the occult.

All of this, then, led me long ago, in my early thirties, to read as much material as I could by Jung and some Jungians. (Jung insisted he wasn't a Jungian!) These books gave me a better understanding of my milieu and myself. Jungian-oriented therapy/analysis also helped me to integrate repressed parts of my personality. No wonder that in my late twenties, like Odysseus, I began my own inner journey, seeking the parts of myself I didn't know yet. And no wonder that at seventy-two I once again chose a Jungian to work with.

TWO

I T'S SYNCHRONISTIC THAT MY FIRST INTERACTIONS WITH DR.
Y occurred in or near bathrooms. I'd been shopping at my
favorite market and using its lavatory when he returned my call
about working with him. As I looked around at the glaring white
porcelain toilet and sink, I recall thinking that it seemed an
appropriate place for us to schedule by phone our first meeting.
Toilets are where we dispose of whatever we've processed in our
digestive tract, material that can be smelly and that we want to
get rid of quickly. Similarly, much of what I would be sharing with
Dr. Y would be things that I didn't want exposed, that could stink
in their own way.

The second bathroom event happened during my first visit to his
office. I needed to use a toilet before we met, and he was exiting the
restroom as I approached it. We nodded at each other, and I was sure
he was my new analyst.

I was right.

While in his waiting room, nervously trying to entertain myself,
I examined all of the framed photographs of doors that hung on
the walls. Anxious about this new potential relationship with an
unfamiliar man, I speculated on opening one of those doors. Where
would it take me? I didn't have an answer, and that uncertainty almost
made me bolt for my car. But I realized Dr. Y and I both would
be opening many doors over the course of our analytic relationship.
This would be just the beginning.

At the appointed time of 2:00 pm, he entered the waiting room
and invited me inside his office. Close to me in age, bearded, and
well over six feet tall, he resembled an Old Testament patriarch. His
calm presence put me at ease immediately. So did his office, located

at the edge of a lagoon, suggesting that we would be working close to the unconscious, often represented symbolically as a body of water. A homey space, his office had a hunter green sofa for patients to sit on and a matching chair for him.

We sat across from each other, and the analysis began when he asked me why I was there. I told him of reading *Man and his Symbols* in 1973 on a camping trip. The book had taken me into a realm I've never left. I also told him about a recent experience I'd had that reminded me of Jung and his ability to perceive what many of us can't.

M and I had visited a Canadian B&B in Osoyoos, British Columbia, owned by expert amateur astronomer Jack Newton, who is recognized worldwide for his publications as well as his images in astrophotography, both in film and CCD. He has a twenty-inch Meade RCX400 telescope. Through it he's able to observe about six hundred stars in the daytime and so much more at night. He gives visitors to his B&B tours through his telescope that are truly mind altering.

While we were there, at intervals in the daytime and evenings, he showed the life teeming around us in the farthest regions of the heavens: stars and planets and nebulae that we normally aren't aware of. Without the aid of a high-powered instrument, our limited vision prevents us from seeing all of these wonders, visible mainly through specialized lenses. This experience reminded me of how much we don't notice as we go about our daily routines and confirmed Hamlet's comment that "There are more things in heaven and earth, Horatio, than are dreamt of in your philosophy." It also confirmed for me that dreams are a kind of telescope, offering a way of penetrating the unknown.

I asked Dr. Y how he had merged the medical (more rational way of being) with the mythic. He said, "I don't see a separation between soma and psyche. Nor did Jung."

Reassured by his response, I told him I'd been in a grocery store bathroom when I'd received his first call. He agreed we'd be spending some of our time in the place where waste products are processed and dispelled.

Then he asked if I'd had any dreams since we'd talked on the phone. I told him of one where I was involved with a group of people who were putting on an impromptu event that included poetry. I seemed to have a leadership role and suggested Robert Hass, a major American poet, as a reader. But several people were down on Hass, claiming that he had turned too conservative. I didn't think that should change the fact that he's a wonderful poet.

I told Dr. Y that Hass represented the more traditional perspective of narrative poetry, and while I also write in that mode, I'm equally drawn to the work of his wife, Brenda Hillman, who tends to be more experimental. I mentioned my own recently published poetry collection, *All This*, and how it blends both worlds. He wondered if Haas represented a more patriarchal view that I continue to favor, though other voices in the dream seem to be challenging me. This could be an issue we'll confront together: the tension between patriarchal consciousness and those voices inside me that oppose it.

He spoke quietly, thoughtfully, making observations about my dreams and other topics without imposing a view. We ranged widely, but our time together also was focused. One of the main themes that surfaced is how to juggle the rational scientific worldview and the mythic. He also wondered if my re-entering therapy could be about a need for renewal, that is, letting go of an old identity and moving toward a new one. He said there might be a lot of resistance to it.

Resistance also could be a reaction to working with a man again. As a younger woman, I'd been in intense therapy with a Jungian-oriented female analyst and established a stronger connection to my feminine roots, among many other things. At seventy-two I felt it would be important to meet with a man. I was sure there must still be many lingering problems to address with a male analyst given that our culture remains so masculine oriented. Men still rule on most levels, and this could be a safe place for me to push back at these inequalities as I more firmly establish my own stance. It's never too late to take on this challenge.

Dr. Y and I conversed easily. I knew before my time was up that I'd found the right person to guide me during this time in my life, wherever that might lead.

THREE

BEFORE MY NEXT SESSION WITH DR. Y, I DREAMT THAT I loved the place where I'd been living and didn't want to move into a new house, which was supposed to have a view of the water. However, the view wasn't enough to make me feel good about making the change, and I wondered if I should have done more to hold onto the previous dwelling. When Dr. Y and I discussed this dream, we agreed it seemed to confirm the internal transformations I would be undergoing in the months ahead. It also suggested I would cling to my more familiar inner structure, my psychic house. The struggle had begun.

It seemed strange to think that at seventy-two, I would shed an old identity as a snake sheds skin. But why should that be surprising? If the *I Ching: The Book of Changes* has any validity, then we're constantly changing, not only physically but also psychologically. Therefore, old age should be as vital a time as any other period in our lives. Snakes shed their skin to allow for further growth, and I was doing something similar. It's true that growth can be scary, and it seems only human to resist change. But I admit to also feeling excited about the possibilities ahead of me. Rather than closing down as I draw closer to the endgame, I may have many other fulfilling things to anticipate.

The following dream appears to confirm the idea that my later years could offer more possibilities than I may have thought. I was gazing into my own eyes, impressed by how brown and clear they were, like looking into absolutely pure, still water. Then the dream zeroed in on my left eye, and I watched in amazement the scenes that unfolded there. The one I recall the most is of different animal species, ones that normally wouldn't get along, hanging out together—lions and sheep, panthers and hyenas.

Dr. Y likened the images to pictures he's seen of Noah's ark that included many species. He also thought the dream hinted at the Great Mother's presence, an archetype that had a strong role in earlier Paleolithic cultures and is associated with nature in all of its manifestations. We continue to experience her today as the force that drives creativity but also brings hurricanes and other natural disasters. Yet she is thought to watch over all that she gives life to, just as animals—humans included—care for their young. This divine female may be appearing in my psyche through these dream images.

After this meeting with Dr. Y and while cooking dinner that night, I started thinking about the dream of my left eye and my analyst's observation about the Great Mother possibly appearing. I imagined being in her arms at night and her protecting me, giving me the nourishment I need. Through these images I saw in that left eye, she transmits the kind of sustenance my own mother was unable to fully convey when I was a child. (As much as I may have appreciated the way Mum embraced life, I harbor lots of regrets that she wasn't a better mother. She abandoned me when I was fourteen and my half-brothers were ten and six, running off with her lover of several years.) These thoughts unleashed a lot of emotion, confirming that I had struck a deep vein. The dream reminded me that I must make room in my days to resonate in this way to my inner world. It takes time for such images to work their way into my heart. I also wanted to draw something of what I saw, to try and capture the dream in more concrete form.

If I could find time.

That seemed to be the major drawback to going deeper, to any major internal change. I was still commuting to the University of San Francisco campus three times a week to teach rhetoric. I also was writing, marketing my work, and managing a household, making it difficult to include activities that could enlarge on my dreams.

Before my next meeting with Dr. Y, I drew an image that had appeared in another dream of women who were creating an arch with their legs for me to pass through. He noted that it resembled a birth passage. Without the drawing, we would not have been aware of this aspect of the dream. He wondered if I were being ushered into the feminine principle in a new way.

That observation made sense given what we'd discussed in previous sessions, but I felt uncomfortable with the abstract term "feminine principle." It wasn't something concrete that I could visualize, though many believe a feminine quality exists in all of humanity, not just in females. According to ancient Chinese philosophers, the yin/yang symbol ☯ is one example where yin (white) represents male energy, and yang (black) conveys the parallel female energy. Yet at this moment in time, when gender identity is being shaken up and the difference between masculine and feminine can no longer be so firmly established biologically, any reference to a feminine principle raises questions and makes me wonder about its role in my psyche. How do I differentiate between feminine and masculine? What am I being initiated into?

When I was writing my novel *Freefall: A Divine Comedy*, this subject came up in one of the scenes I created. Tillie, the point-of-view character, an installation artist, reflects on it:

> She knows there's a lot of talk in certain circles about matriarchies and patriarchies and "the feminine" and "the masculine." But what do these words mean? Has masculine consciousness so dominated Western thought that it's impossible to tease out what might be feminine? If women can't locate the source of their being, and if they view themselves through masculine constructs and lenses, then how can they ever truly know themselves? It's a problem Tillie has struggled with for a long time: How do women find their true identities in a mostly male world?

Clearly, it's also something that I've wrestled with over the years. Perhaps, as I'm aging, there is something in my feminine self that is lacking and needs reinforcing. I've read that as men age, their female aspects become more pronounced, and the opposite can be true for women. Am I taking a different route? Or maybe it isn't either/or. I've never been in doubt about my female identity, though people called me a tomboy when I was a girl because I loved to explore and do things associated with boys, like climbing cliffs or borrowing my uncle's bike so I could explore Calgary and beyond. I also have worshiped what males take for granted, their inherent physical power and acquired cultural influence. They still control most of our institutions. Why wouldn't I want the same influence? Such control can be a tremendous lure.

This female imagery came up in another dream of a young woman who was somewhat overweight—plump. She appeared in a "lucid dream," one during which I was totally awake in the dream and conscious of dreaming. I pinched her, wanting to see if she were real, but she didn't have any material substance. A hazy dream figure urged me to stay in touch with this girl/woman. (Was the dream figure punning?) Several "Lilys" also inhabited this scenario, sitting in different positions around the room. Five aspects of myself.

Later that morning, while riding our stationary bike and simultaneously reading an article on the Japanese writer Haruki Murakami's desire to show how reality and fiction leak into each other via his narratives, I thought about the woman from the lucid dream and the admonition to stay in touch with her. Something about this woman made me start sobbing. Who is she? She resembled a big doll or an oversized, overstuffed girl. Feminine for sure. And moonlike. When I finished biking, I floated out of our exercise room on a flood of tears and began writing about her.

The Moon Maiden

I first met the moon maiden in a dream. She was a little overweight and also a little removed, not someone I would sit down and chat with. Externally, she resembled one of those Russian dolls that collapse inside each other, and I was surprised that she didn't seem to have any substance. No real flesh to grasp. I lifted her skirt, wondering what was beneath it, but she was fully covered by a pair of old-fashioned white cotton briefs like my mother used to wear.

It surprised me that someone in the dream had urged me to keep in touch with this young woman. Why? She seemed bland, unevolved, distant. Disconnected from my daily reality. Why was she so important that a dream visit had made me aware of her?

When I thought about the girl later, her round shape reminded me of the moon, and I came to think of her as the "moon maiden." She did seem otherworldly. A little untouchable. But she has touched me in some way (as I touched her in the dream?) because I keep thinking of her. So even if I don't know exactly where she exists or why she visited, she has penetrated (ironically, with that round shape) me enough that I can't get her out of my mind. Is her appearance a response to my confusion about the "feminine principle," suggesting that this maid is some aspect of it?

If she is an emissary from the moon, a real moon maiden, then she must share some of its qualities: the ability to go through phases as we women do with our menstrual cycles. A mysterious dark side that can appear and disappear at times. Self-possessed. Mysterious. Some nights the moon can be brilliant and flood the dark with its milky light. On others, it turns away, carrying on in some private manner, leaving the earth to care for itself.

How was I going to keep in touch with this mutable young woman if I wasn't sure where to find her? She seems to be shadowing me, not coming fully into view, a little like the moon when it is going through a dark phase. One of these nights, I expect she'll appear in another dream. Perhaps I'll recognize her not because of my experience of her in the original dream but as someone who wants to teach me something, to lead me into the dark side of the moon, away from the sun's bright light.

Certainly, getting old calls up images of the moon's dark side. It has a desolate quality to it just as old age often does for some people. Later, I wondered if some aspect of the moon maiden had surfaced from my current reading about Inanna, the ancient Sumerian goddess of love, beauty, war, justice, political power, and sex. Is there some aspect of the moon maiden in the Inanna material? Inanna seems to be taking me closer to the moon's mysteries. Sylvia Brinton Perera's *Descent to the Goddess: A Way of Initiation for Women* describes her descent to the underworld. Just as the star Venus descends in the west and reappears in the east each night, Inanna also lived according to the moon's cycles rather than the sun's. Is this what I should be focusing on more now, this more feminine way of living and perceiving? But what kind of changes would that require of me?

Time is the major barrier to developing a deeper connection with myself via dreams and otherwise. So many things are drawing my attention in multiple directions: for a start, those five Lilys I saw in a dream that I mentioned earlier. Each of these parts wants to be noticed, acknowledged, and developed further. Each wants to be heard. As a writer, I also, daily, must honor my vocation. To write is as important to me as food. It is food, nourishing me emotionally, spiritually, and intellectually. Through the imagination, it's one of the ways I sustain contact with myself on multiple levels, hence, I'm sure, the five Lilys. (I believe there actually are more than five!) By writing poetry, fiction, memoir, travel pieces, essays, and more, as well as dabbling in the visual arts—mainly watercolors, acrylics, and mixed media—I'm constantly stimulated, engaging my inner and outer worlds on multiple levels.

But it's difficult when day-to-day routines, including my writing, take over, and I have little time left for what surfaces in other ways from the underworld.

FOUR

A s I WRITE ABOUT AGING, I KEEP ASKING MYSELF ABOUT MY goals. In part, I hope that reflecting on my final years will help me to better understand this last stage and deepen it. Writing about getting older will force me to look more closely at my days in that light. Perhaps, in sharing this progression, my readers will make their own discoveries, as has been true for me whenever I've read about someone else's journey. Also, *Dreaming Myself into Old Age* involves various modes of dreaming, not just night dreams. Art is an important part of this journey, including the art of teaching.

Yet I also believe that aging offers its own mysteries for us to uncover, and that is part of my quest here as well. There isn't just one way to age well. Nor is there a formula to fit everyone. We all must find the path that works for us. So, in writing about this time in my life, I'm not just interested in how I encounter each day. I want more than that. I hope to dig deeper into this perplexing journey toward death that we're all involved in from birth. It's too easy to become buried in daily minutia and therefore miss what's really important.

During our younger years, we're caught up in work, finding partners (or not), raising kids (if we've decided to have them), and establishing ourselves in the world. The focus is outward and not so much on our inner life. However, once we've moved past those demands, we have opportunities to explore our interior realm. Aging thoughtfully, then, includes opening up more to our fantasies and dreams, our memories and reveries, especially as the outer world closes down, and we gradually must withdraw from activities that once came easily to us.

This has already happened to me. Until I was seventy-five or so, I had no problem loading my mountain bike onto our car's bike rack and taking a spin. But the fear of falling and breaking something caused me to stop my periodic outdoor biking and limit myself to taking walks along the water and using our stationary bike on other days.

Yet turning inward doesn't mean we need to renounce just having fun. Those experiences are equally important. Traveling to new or revisiting old places is still possible, whether in actuality or via TV/Netflix/video. An eighty-three-year-old friend recently told me about a virtual reality experience her granddaughter had introduced her to. My friend said, "I wasn't interested in some new digital toy." Skeptical of entering this realm, she resisted it at first. But she didn't want to disappoint her granddaughter and finally gave in. She said, "It was transcendent, the most amazing experience I've ever had! I felt as if I were actually walking along a path on this mountain trail. Everything looked so vivid and real. More real, in a way, than in actual life. I was in full control of what I did there." She can't wait to do it again.

Someone who has traveled the world in her younger days and still takes trips, my friend has found a new way to experience places she can no longer manage physically. She can visit Antarctica without freezing to death; descend to the floor of the Grand Canyon without moving her feet; climb Mount Everest with no risk of falling; explore the Hermitage museum in St. Petersburg and even get a close-up look at the paintings; or hang out in India without being besieged by beggars. These simulations offer immersive experiences that users can interact with and explore without moving from their chairs. In other words, the viewer controls the environment; has the power to look around at any scene; and can, potentially, interact with the objects in the scene. It simulates a place in the real world that a person can enter and leave at any time by using special technology. Of course, dreams also offer an opportunity to travel to new places. I've visited Russia, Japan, France, and so many other places in my dreams!

For the less adventurous, fun can still be had by sharing good food and wine with friends and acquaintances. It needn't involve hosting elaborate dinner parties but can be more informal. Appetizers are easy to put together for "happy hours" at home with our friends. Attending concerts and plays. Visiting museums. Reading absorbing books. Dancing, even if we can only do it in our wheelchairs by moving our bodies to the music's rhythms.

Yet entertainment needn't exclude analysis and thought. It needn't be either/or. Both approaches energize and inspire me.

Some people might think we'll be the same as we age as we've always been. This could be true, and, of course, it's okay if people don't want to evolve, which requires change. However, it's never too late to make overdue modifications in our lives, to awaken to ways in which we delude ourselves, as King Lear realizes and as I discovered in the dream I mentioned earlier during which my husband was driving the car but looking to the left rather than at the road. I wouldn't have known about my allegiance to rules being a problem in the dream world, as well as externally, if I hadn't recorded the dream and further investigated it. I believe old age offers as rich a time of learning and growing as our younger years did, a time of discovering who we are in the fullest sense. I know that I'm still making important discoveries about myself and those around me. I look forward to making many more!

FIVE

Early in 2004, I published "*Mundus Imaginalis: Reflections after Seeing Magritte*" in the *San Francisco Jung Institute Library Journal*. The term *mundus imaginalis* originated with Henry Corbin, a philosopher, theologian, Iranologist, and professor of Islamic studies at the École Pratique des Hautes Études in Paris. He had coined *mundus imaginalis* because he thought the term "imaginary" suggested something that isn't real, yet when he used imaginary, he meant something quite different. Corbin needed another word so he didn't confuse western readers who might be studying his erudite and metaphysical texts. *Mundus imaginalis* signifies a totally different kind of reality than what we in the West might conjure up. For him, *mundus imaginalis* conveyed the imaginative consciousness, something that was real to Corbin.

I told Dr. Y that Corbin's ideas remind me of the eye dream I described earlier and how what I see from my left eye doesn't necessarily reach consciousness. But I believe it offers an opening into Corbin's world, one that Dr. Y is familiar with. I may not be able to experience that dimension directly, yet much of my poetry and some of my fiction connects me to it. In my writing, I attempt to answer the questions: What is reality? How can art and artists help us to understand it?

I'm grateful that Dr. Y has helped me to connect with this realm again. It's terribly important to me. It IS me! It's beyond soul. It isn't just my soul, but it carries my soul and me. It may be why museums have become my places of worship—museums and plays and concerts and literature. Art is the one way I can understand what Henry Corbin is writing about.

Here, then, is the piece that articulates my perceptions, my essay that the *San Francisco Jung Journal* published early in the twenty-first century:

Mundus Imaginalis: Reflections After Seeing Magritte

"Omissions are not accidents." —Marianne Moore

Since seeing the Magritte show at San Francisco's MOMA in July 2000, I've been thinking more about the relationship between painting and poetry: each reveals (or conceals) reality, remaking it either on the canvas or the page. As a poet, I've been conscious of how poetry can interrogate appearances, things, and ideas, aware of how language shapes and reshapes our perceptions.

Magritte had a similar understanding. In his painting *Ceci n'est pas une pipe (This is not a pipe)*, he's pointing out, of course, that this particular pipe he has painted isn't actually a pipe, but he's also questioning whether what we name is actually what we name. The pipe depicted on the canvas, though realistically painted, isn't a pipe but instead is his conception of one. You can't smoke it. You can't hold it. Its reality only exists on the canvas. You could call it anything—a made-up word—cetek, for example, as long as others agreed with your meaning. Therefore, it isn't a pipe.

In other experiments with language and image, Magritte drew "vaguely biomorphic forms" on canvas and then wrote words inside the shapes, such as *l'arbre* (tree), *le nuage* (cloud), *le ciel* (sky), *la montagne* (mountain). (*Magritte.* San Francisco, San Francisco Museum of Modern Art, 2000, p. 15) The shape is not related to the word and even at times contradicts it. In one painting the emblem for mountain loosely resembles moose antlers. Magritte shows viewers how dependent we are on the words themselves to create the images we see, when in actuality they also are not the thing they describe. The word tree is not a tree. It only points to a shared meaning.

In his painting *The Human Condition*, it first appears that we're looking through a window at a pastoral scene. Then we notice that the view through the window isn't seamless. Our eye catches on the edge of a canvas that's set up in front of the window, and then we become aware that the canvas is sitting on an easel. Initially, it appears as if a "painter" within the painting—a stand-in for Magritte—has created the scene in the picture, there being an almost seamless movement from canvas to what can be viewed through the window.

Magritte has created the illusion that the image depicted in the painting shows what the artist is working on, and we've walked in on that event. But as viewers, we're also aware that the outdoor scene is an extension of the actual canvas we're looking at. The artist has manipulated us into thinking we're seeing an accurate representation of a scene when we're being shown quite the opposite. We've been duped. Art takes on the appearances of reality. It gives us another view of reality; it teases us into thinking it is reality—without being actually real. A gap always exists between the words we use to name reality and reality itself, leaving room for misunderstandings, confusion, mystery, and especially wonder.

Adrienne Gagnon, who helped curate the Magritte show, says, "Magritte painted in the chasm between our vision of the world and the world itself, between our attempts to rationalize every phenomenon, and the absurdity that continues to pervade life despite all effort to suppress it." He did not shy away from this absurdity. Rather, he sought it in his work—a woman's long red hair appearing to flow out of a pair of shoes, another pair of shoes turning into the feet wearing them (or vice versa).

Paul Klee was onto this gap in our experience as well. In an excerpt from his writing in another SFMOMA show, he says:

> In our time worlds have opened up which not everybody can see into, although they too are part of nature ... An in-between world. At least for me it's an in-between world. I call it that because I feel that it exists between the worlds our senses can perceive, and I absorb it inwardly to the extent that I can project it outwardly in symbolic correspondences. Children, madmen, and savages can still, or again, look into it. And what they see and picture is for me the most precious kind of confirmation. For we all see the same things but from different angles.

Many poets write poems that function in a similar way, sharing Magritte's (and Klee's) fascination with how artists convey reality, questioning whether it even can be rendered with paint or with words, acting in the gap between art and life. This gap seems to be the source of some deeper truth or way of seeing that art can investigate, an attempt to get to what's real. Or, as Marianne Moore asked in an essay she once wrote for *The Dial*, "Is the Real the Actual?"

There's another way of approaching this question. We could label what we see with our limited, waking perception as secondary reality as some Buddhists do—the world of Maya or illusion. Primary reality, less readily available to us, is what dreams and some art can convey, more real in their way than appearances—an in-between world.

Again, I'm thinking here of the Magritte paintings I recently saw. Several of his images take place inside a room, an enclosed space often overwhelmed with what it contains— an apple that looks about to burst, filling the room it's in, the windows on the left a welcome relief from an otherwise claustrophobic setting. Or one of his more famous ones—*Les Valeurs Personnelles* (Personal Values)—where you're looking inside a room whose walls are painted to give the illusion of a blue sky filled with cumulous clouds. Nothing is where it should be (the sky is not in the sky but inside an enclosed space), and the objects defy being contained by our ideas of them. Several are either over or undersized, leaving the viewer feeling slightly off balance: What is that enlarged comb doing leaning on the wall, propped on the miniature bed, the comb almost as tall as the ceiling? Who lives in this space? Where are we?

Neither of these paintings tells us much about secondary reality, other than it isn't what interests Magritte, at least not ultimately, though it can be manipulated to suggest almost anything. But they do allude to what lies behind our notions of the world around us, suggesting that these everyday objects we take for granted—an oversized wine glass, shaving brush, matchstick, and comb, all resting on two Persian carpets— carry deeper meanings. Are these magic carpets directly from the world of the Arabian Nights, carrying the room aloft into the blue skies of the imagination? Are we locked inside a dream of Magritte's? Or has he freed us from the prison of more conventional appearances?

The picture reminds me of William Carlos Williams' much-anthologized poem "The Red Wheelbarrow"[2] where he also presents his personal values, different from Magritte's, but similar in the notion of no ideas but in things:

> so much depends
> upon
> a red wheel
> barrow
> glazed with rain
> water
> beside the white
> chickens

Magritte's "things" reverberate within their enclosed space, just as the red wheelbarrow does in the frame of the poem, larger than life—encapsulating life itself. However, poets depend not just on red wheelbarrows, the literal level of a word's meaning, but on the connotative level as well. The literal may draw us in, but it's the mix of the two that creates new meanings, that can lift a poem from mere documentation to something else.

Language has even more plasticity than paint or clay because it functions on so many levels. Not only do we have an alphabet that can be combined in countless ways to form multiple meanings, but we also have the sound of each letter and word, agreed-on definitions, the coloring that tone gives to our expressions, phrasing, emphasis, memories, ideas, and a reader's associations. It's a potent mix that can create subtle though powerful effects in the right hands. As Magritte reminds us, language—the veil through which we apprehend the world—seems the most mysterious medium. In their very elusiveness, if we are sensitive to their fluctuations of meaning and description, words constantly challenge our perceptions. They only appear to be what they say they are, as Magritte has shown us. They actually are slippery conveyors of reality and not absolutely dependable.

Some artists, visual and literary, attempt to jolt us out of our usual way of seeing in the way they use their particular medium to challenge what we take to be real. The degree to which a work does shake us up may even be a measure of its success. This attempt to shock viewers/readers into new ways of seeing or experiencing isn't new.

Before the language poets (and others who dislocate language to challenge our usual way of seeing and experiencing) arrived on the scene, Marianne Moore was using collage, appropriating language and imagery wherever she could find it—catalogues, newspapers, magazines, journals, books, the visual arts—to create her "imaginary gardens with real toads in them."[3] Bonnie Costello, in her discussion of "Moore and the Visual Arts," says, "Reality is not simply replaced by the canvas; it is reinvented there."[4] I think this observation can be applied to certain poems as well, of Moore's and others.

This impulse to reinvent reality has been with us for so long—I'm thinking of the caves at Lascaux and other archeological findings where early Homo sapiens have left their mark—that there must be an urgent need for humans to do it. Could it be these depictions are like another layer of skin that unite us collectively? Would we be unable to recognize ourselves without this archetypal layer?

It's a provocative idea that some artists are reinventing reality, that perhaps we're dependent on them to help us see more clearly and deeply, that as viewers (and readers) we participate in this invention and internalize the results. If it's true, then it causes me to look at art differently, literary and visual, seeking more than just an aesthetic experience.

Marianne Moore's poem "An Octopus"[5] lets us know from the beginning that we're in for a shock:

An Octopus

of ice. Deceptively reserved and flat,
it lies 'in grandeur and in mass'
beneath a sea of shifting snow dunes;
dots of cyclamen-red and maroon on its clearly defined
pseudo-podia
made of glass that will bend—a much-needed invention—

comprising twenty-eight ice-fields from fifty to five hundred
feet thick,
of unimagined delicacy.

Our first shock after reading this poem? It isn't about an
octopus at all. But we don't learn until well into it what the
real subject is, Mount Tacoma, though even that location is
questionable: The mountain isn't exactly Mount Tacoma, but
a replica that Moore has created for her own purposes, to
show the reader how elusive and/or allusive language is—
and how suggestive:

Completing a circle,
you have been deceived into thinking that you have
          progressed,
under the polite needles of the larches
"hung to filter, not to intercept the sunlight"—

As readers, we've been deluded into thinking that we've
progressed under Moore's polite use of language (her formal
tone), each new image and idea needling us. The whole poem
is "deceptively reserved and flat" beneath a shifting sea of
language, throwing up onto the shore of the page the flotsam
and jetsam of borrowed thoughts, adding up to a totally
new reality from what they originally intended. The words
have been radically displaced and relocated, creating new
meanings.

Constructed from language appropriated from sources as
wide-ranging as "The Rockies of Canada," words overheard
at a circus, Ruskin, *London Graphic*, Cardinal Newman's
Historical Sketches, The Five Great Philosophies, "An Octopus"—
like any work of art worth the name—becomes a many-sided
creature, whose complexities will "still be complexities /
as long as the world lasts." Greek rationality cannot resolve the
conundrums in the poem (nor in life or art): "The Greeks
liked smoothness, distrusting what was back / of what could
not be clearly seen."

But Moore wants us to be aware of what's hidden from
view, secondary and primary reality reflected in the lines
"the mountain guide evolving from the trapper, / 'in two pairs

of trousers, the outer one older, / wearing slowly away from the feet to the knees'." The outer trousers, secondary reality, are wearing away, as are the ideas associated with them that delude us into thinking this octopus of a mountain is innocent. Moore warns us to beware of

> Neatness of finish! Neatness of finish!
> Relentless accuracy is the nature of this octopus
> with its capacity for fact.
> "Creeping slowly as with meditated stealth,
> its arms seeming to approach from all directions,"
> it receives one under winds that "tear the snow to bits
> and hurl it like a sandblast
> shearing off twigs and loose bark from the trees."

Yet can language be trusted? "Is 'tree' the word for these things / 'flat on the ground like vines'?" This deceptively "rational" world of facts can turn on us, creating an illusion of safety, the mountain a mere façade for the potential violence within, "its top a complete cone like Fujiyama's / till an explosion blew it off."

In "The Monkey Puzzle,"[6] Moore's subject is again elusive, quicksilver in its changes:

> A kind of monkey or pine-lemur
> not of interest to the monkey,
> in a kind of Flaubert's Carthage, it defies one—
> this "Paduan cat with lizard," this "tiger in a bamboo
>   thicket."
> "An interwoven somewhat," it will not come out.
> Ignore the Foo dog and it is forthwith more than a dog,
> its tail superimposed upon itself in a complacent half spiral,
> this pine-tree—this pine-tiger, is a tiger, not a dog.

Moore actually may have been inspired to write this poem by a Rousseau painting since "she drew formal and conceptual inspiration" from modern painting. She often revisioned what visual artists from the past have seen, painting and poetry no longer bound "to a strict imitation of nature" (if that ever was truly possible). Since Moore takes much of her material from pictures rather than from life, "her visual representations are at one remove from nature—the world they construct already interpreted." This approach suggests she found paintings more real than reality, or truer. In Costello's words, "Since 'sight' is hampered by convention, 'insight' is necessary."

Conventional seeing has a hard time getting a foothold in "The Monkey Puzzle." The subject of the poem is a puzzle, "a kind of monkey or pine lemur." Whatever it is, "it will not come out," located in another artist's construct, "Flaubert's Carthage," a product of the imagination. Moore's forms are not of nature, not representational, but of the imagination. Like so much of modern art, the poem is its own reality—not a mirror or imitation.

The crystal represents Moore's preferred way of perceiving reality, also providing "the cubists with a major metaphor of their new art." The crystal's various angles cause us to be aware of its multifaceted surface and its inner core simultaneously. Moore's poems move in a similar way, giving the reader the illusion of seeing "a thing from all sides, giving an impression of infinity to a finite subject."

Costello goes on to say that "Moore adopts from painters the double sense of looking at something. The impulse to find a conceptual unity within the visual multiplicity is one she shares with modernist painters. Her note from M. Krohgon on futurists could stand for her own work: 'the Futurist . . . has got to see feel understand and interpret the front side and the back side of things, the inside as well as the outside and the bottom as well as or better than the top.'"

More important for my discussion here, Moore, a contemporary of Magritte (he died in 1967, she in 1972), was equally fascinated with how the real can quickly become strange with just a few slight strokes. Her poem "The Magician's Retreat" aptly draws the parallel:

The Magician's Retreat
of moderate height,
(I have seen it)
cloudy but bright inside
like a moonstone,
while a yellow glow

from a shutter-crack shone,
and a blue glow from the lamppost
close to the front door.
It left nothing of which to complain,
nothing more to obtain,
consummately plain.
A black tree mass rose at the back
almost touching the eaves
with the definiteness of Magritte,
was above all discreet.

Costello points out that Moore took the title for the poem
from an "eighteenth-century drawing by Jean Jacques Lequeu
but describes a painting by Magritte called 'Dominion of
Lights.' The two pictures are very similar but use inverse
effects of light and dark."

The painting itself has an eerie quality, like its sister of
the same name painted in 1952 but with subtle shifts in mood.
The lamplight in the earlier painting casts a warmer, more
welcoming yellow light; in the 1961 version, the lamplight has
a bluish cast, as described in Moore's poem.

A middle-class family home built early in the twentieth
century or late in the nineteenth, the house does look
ordinary at first. But after studying the painting, the house
feels as if it's under a spell: it could be a magician's retreat.
(Perhaps magician could be another name for the artist.)
The windows reveal nothing about the interior of the place,
the orangey-yellow light appearing to bleed through blinds
covering the second-story windows that conceal whatever
may be happening within. The lower windows are hidden
behind closed shutters. If there's a front entry to the house,
it's in the shadows.

In fact, much of "The Dominion of Light" takes place
in shadow, the lower half of the painting all in darkness,
suggesting the middle of the night, except for the single lit
lamppost, casting "a blue glow" and the lights shining from
inside the house. The blue sky—as light as midday, filled
with light-filled cumulus clouds—seems totally out of place
in this painting. How can day and night exist simultaneously?
Where is this house?

In Moore's poem, she sees the house as complete in itself, perfect in its consummate plainness. And it does give off the feeling of something uncanny, for Freud a signal of the unconscious, able to keep its dark secrets in the midst of so much light pressing down on it. The black tree mass blocking out part of the darkened house and the brightly lit sky is the one element in the painting unifying sky, earth, and house, retaining the blackness of the lower half, even when its leaves and branches are silhouetted against the blue sky. Discreet, yes, and definite, contrasting the mechanical light from the lamppost and within the house to the natural light in the sky.

It's true that Moore has "seen" this magician's retreat, as she states in the poem, and, with Magritte, lives under its magical cloak, able to create imaginal worlds where day and night seem to co-exist, recreating reality to serve their art. Both artists challenge us to let go of our conventional expectations (secondary reality), offering a way to draw closer to the real.

SIX

FROM WHAT I'VE WRITTEN SO FAR, IT MAY SOUND AS IF I float around on a cloud of dreams and wild ideas fed by Jungian psychology with no connection to everyday reality. Not so! None of this soul searching and groping for meaning has taken place in a vacuum. Far from it. And as I've already said, the everyday demands tend to overshadow the subliminal ones, usually taking precedent. I live most of my days in secondary reality.

The first thing I do when I wake up is write down my dreams and spend a few minutes thinking about them. On mornings when I have time, I meditate for twenty minutes or so before having breakfast. From then on, I'm fully engaged in whatever the day brings, which can include planning menus, putting in my daily writing session, marketing the works I've already published or sending out shorter pieces for publication, doing my daily aerobic workout on our stationary bike, teaching, grocery shopping, cooking dinner, and whatever else is on my plate that day.

I also must deal daily with whatever anxieties have visited me. Since childhood, I've had a healthy share of fears and started smoking cigarettes before I was eleven to tamp them down. Fortunately, I quit in my late twenties. Otherwise, I might not be alive today. Though I've learned to manage my response to these worries, they still flare up and remind me of my many vulnerabilities, including my concerns about aging and the deterioration to mind and body that accompanies it.

This poem of mine reflects some of my feelings about what I'm dealing with:

> Age cuts into us
> Our skin doesn't resist

Time loves crevices
it can hide inside

*

I don't recognize this woman
whose skin sags and has lost
its purpose leaving me longing
for something I can't articulate

the way a child can be at loss
for words because she hasn't found them yet
and I haven't found the words I need
to explain why I'm having
so much trouble
aging

*

What do I have to lose if I shed
this façade that doesn't resemble me
any longer and dive into one
of those crevices in my face or worry
lines between my brows
and disappear

Each day, I must face whatever anxieties have surfaced that reflect my ongoing concerns. I still get mammograms, and when I notice a twinge in one of my breasts, my first thought is CANCER. I then have to talk myself out of whatever panic has briefly taken over and thrown me into despair. This fear of breast cancer will never completely leave. My mammograms show that I have what are called dense breasts, and, apparently, they are more susceptible to cancer because the density hides incipient tumors. Like most women, I feel enormously protective of these organs, one part of my body that announces my most feminine self. No wonder I fear losing them.

Of course, my body has more parts than my breasts, and I'm hyperalert to its many twinges and pains, concerned that at any moment I'll face, as my husband did, an unexpected and possibly life-threatening illness. Fortunately, this attitude is countered by its opposite: the belief that I'll live forever! It can be difficult to reconcile these two extremes in myself. And while I'm susceptible to many health fears, I'm actually not a hypochondriac and usually only visit a doctor for my yearly checkups.

At seventy-two, I was still employed by the University of San Francisco (USF) as an adjunct professor in rhetoric and language, with two classes each semester of mainly first-year men and women, a post I'd held for over thirty years. (I also was vice-president of the Part-Time Faculty Association.) I scheduled my classes midday. That meant I didn't have to battle the morning commute traffic from San Francisco's East Bay into the city, but it was still an hour drive each way. I liked the classroom dynamic enough to continue working with youth until 2015. Also, teaching them to think critically and write clearly seemed an important contribution to sustaining a working democracy. And, an equal opportunity feminist, I enjoyed having my own income so I could contribute financially to our household.

But at seventy-five, I left my post as a union rep and quit teaching undergraduates. Reading and grading over two hundred papers a semester of varying lengths had lost its glow, though I still loved helping people to become better writers. Now, the creative writing workshops I offer to older adults at USF's Fromm Institute for Lifelong Learning are the most satisfying teaching experience I've ever had. Grades aren't necessary, and that removes me as judge-in-chief of students' work. They know their submissions can't fail, so they're freer in what they try to write, taking risks they might not have done if a grade was waiting for them.

At the Fromm, I've had the privilege of working with individuals who are still fully engaged in life, ranging in age from their late fifties to midnineties. It's fully rewarding to create classes that take them into new territory and to witness them incorporating elements in their prose that I've introduced them to in our workshops. The drafts they bring to our sessions for peer critiques and my own feedback show them building their writer's toolbox and discovering the areas they need to develop. Ever a student, I, of course, learn as much as they do. For each of the classes I teach at the Fromm, I do extensive research and continue to deepen my knowledge of the writer's craft. In a way, I'm my own best learner! In any field, there's always room to expand, deepen, and improve.

I'm also a good role model for my Fromm students since in 2015, at age seventy-five, I was a "debut" novelist with *Fling!*, a narrative I'd been writing and revising for many years, which makes the "debut" part humorous if not ludicrous. Since then, I've published three more novels: *Curva Peligrosa, Freefall: A Divine Comedy,* and *The Ripening: A Canadian Girl Grows Up,* a sequel to *Freefall*; and a poetry chapbook: *No More Kings.* In 2011, Little Red Tree Publishing released my 129-page poetry collection, *All This.* I've demonstrated that creativity can have a long shelf life and isn't something we necessarily retire from.

My classes usually meet in the Fromm seminar room, the right size for a group of twenty-five students, though that number whittles down to between seventeen and nineteen. Some attendees may have scheduled trips that interrupt our eight-week workshop, but since I send them pdf copies of the presentations for each session—the slides containing the main elements I want to cover on that day—they can still keep up with what we're doing.

There are several tables, large enough for four or five students to sit around, and I seat them with different people for each class. That way, when they meet in small groups for peer critique sessions, they eventually will connect with everyone directly. This format also gives them a wide array of responses to their drafts, so they're not stuck with the same perspective every meeting.

When we discuss a reading I've passed out, I wander the room with the mic while the hands of those who want to respond to the piece shoot into the air, many of their insights truly illuminating. Very few withhold their input during this part of the class.

These students genuinely enjoy not only exploring their own experiences in writing, but they also love reading their class members' drafts. It's a rich learning experience for everyone, including me, since they all are wonderfully vocal and thoughtful.

But the most exciting part of teaching writing to older adults is the community that forms—an essential part of most educational institutions that serve seniors. They love telling and listening to one another's stories, which sparks their own memories, all of which leads to more writing and sharing. They also discover how others near them in age are coping with the challenges of growing older. For me, it's been doubly inspiring to read their work and participate in this stage of their lives in such a meaningful way.

Though teaching is how I contribute financially to our household, my real work is writing, something few people make a living at. (Only 5 percent of writers can support themselves from publishing books.) Since remarrying in 1994, my schedule has been full. Still, while teaching and handling all of the other demands on my time, I somehow have found an hour each day during which to write and, as I've already mentioned, I've created four novels and countless poems, short stories, and articles that I've published widely. The truth is, writing is as essential to me as eating. If I don't practice it each day, I can become irritable and unpleasant to live with.

In many ways, writing and teaching are similar for me. Both are creative activities that give me an opportunity to investigate ideas, fears, interests, and obsessions—to ask and answer questions. The two roles complement each other, writing being a more introverted activity than teaching. When I write, I do the dance of the seven veils. I remain relatively hidden while also exposing myself, exploring my mind and imagination in public view (as I'm doing here), trying to tempt the reader into entering the domain I'm creating. When I teach, I do a similar dance. Some seduction is needed to motivate others to write since for many it's a vexed activity. Those older adults who struggled to produce papers in grade school and college carry that memory lifelong, so I need to encourage them to try it again without seeming too maternal.

At the Fromm Institute, I've taught memoir as well as flash non-fiction, scene creation, and personal essay. Memoir and fiction both require similar skills: each uses narrative to tell a story. As a writer, I'm constantly trying to master different aspects of the writing craft since there are always more to discover. Since learning new things and being engaged deeply in life can foster a richer, more satisfying old age, I'm grateful that both my writing and my teaching contribute substantially to that goal.

I've seen other seniors at the Fromm benefit profoundly from what the institution offers. One man, whom I'll call Tom, has taken all of my classes. His eyesight and hearing are failing, so he sits near the front. He also has slowed down in his ability to follow mentally what I'm covering in class. But he still has some wonderful comments on the readings we discuss; his own writing tends to be wry and studded with humor, the latter being an essential quality to get through these later years successfully. I often see him walking haltingly to his car, using a couple of canes for stability, and my heart soars to think that he continues to make the effort to expand his horizons, even though he's confronting major afflictions. All of my students inspire me and give me hope.

SEVEN

I N 1984, ONE OF THE REQUIRED CLASSES FOR MY MASTER'S IN humanities degree (my first MA) was a seminar taught by Joseph Axelrod, author of *The University Teacher as Artist*, now a classic text. A graduate of the University of Chicago and strongly influenced by Robert Hutchins, the famous American educator, Axelrod had a lifelong interest in education. He also had served as a consultant for several emerging academic programs. Two of them, the Academy of Art College in San Francisco and World College West—an innovative four-year liberal arts college that ran out of funding in 1992—asked Axelrod to shape their liberal arts programs and to advise faculty.

I didn't know much about him then. I knew he taught both comparative literature and the humanities at San Francisco State. But I wasn't aware of his interest in education. Nor did I know that he would become a major mentor for me, my guide into teaching. At that point, I just wanted the liberal arts focus of the humanities to give me a better foundation as a writer. I hadn't expected to combine writing with teaching when I graduated.

During my final year in that program, Axelrod oversaw my thesis, a combination analytic and creative work. Simultaneously, I applied for a job teaching expository writing at World College West. Because of Axelrod's recommendation, World College West invited me to teach my first class there in 1984. The following semester, I also was appointed to teach Oral and Written English under his direction at the Academy of Art College.

Suddenly, I was thrust into being an instructor, scrambling to educate myself in the then-new ideas about the writing process and the most effective ways of teaching college-level writing. Not only was I diving into the world of rhetoric, giving myself a crash course, but I had never heard of a cumulative or periodic sentence. Nor could I tell the difference between a noun phrase and a relative clause. I wrote intuitively, having absorbed grammar and its rules over the years without being able to articulate them consciously. Now I needed to quickly learn these things so I could explain them to students, building my base as a teacher and writer.

I couldn't have asked for better training. Teaching others has helped me to remove some of the veils that otherwise would have kept me from mastering the craft of writing. It has forced me to understand the basics of a well-constructed sentence and the abundance of choices I have as a writer. I've learned it is more difficult to consciously break the rules if you don't know them.

Similarly, my own forays as a writer have made me a better writing teacher. I'm more aware of the many pitfalls and joys of writing. I also have discovered how important it is for writers to find their own voice—and trust it. I teach from that stance. I don't make rigid rules, such as prohibiting the use of the second person pronoun or any of the other inhibiting injunctions many of us learned in grade school and later. Rather, I ask students to examine what they say within the context of what they're writing. The only firm rule is that audience and purpose determine approach, no matter what genre they're working in. Knowing that I'm a practicing writer myself, students are more likely to take me seriously. But I'm learning, too, from their successes and failures, growing along with my students as a teacher and writer.

However, growth requires a willingness to try new things, both on the teacher's part and the student's, and an atmosphere in which such risks can take place. According to Axelrod, taking risks is one of the arts that the teacher-artist uses. All the great artists at teaching have made discoveries as they go—even Socrates. He didn't form the opus alone. Every member of the group who entered into a relationship with him during the discussion created it. Something mysterious happens with a group that's meeting for a shared purpose, turning a collection of individuals into an entity that transcends itself, making some classes fly and others never get off the ground.

A dream I had speaks to this situation. A former creative writing teacher of mine, M. H., was with me when a couple of female students showed up, excited about some inventive and ambitious projects they'd decided to do. One woman had created a kind of book for everyone in the class, making it all by hand, though I don't recall exactly what its contents were. I just remember thinking in the dream that it was very imaginative. Another student made huge stuffed animals that functioned as cushions in the classroom for students to lean on. A third student was thrilled because I'd managed to locate some Yamaha pianos for them to use.

I felt some obligation to explain to M. H. that these students were involved in these visual arts for cultural studies, though what I mainly teach is expository writing, as if I had to apologize for their unorthodox work. M. H., whose influence on me wasn't positive when I was her student—I felt she was overly critical—was really impressed with these students' enthusiasm, a surprising reaction from her. And I was proud of them, delighted I'd been able to provide the space for them to experiment.

This dream shows an acceptance from this more critical M. H. aspect of myself, one of my internal censors. I'm able to let these students explore their own interests, each in his or her own way, in this case, my own developing learners. Most importantly, the scene shows how students can form a safe and inviting place for each other, this one young woman giving her fellow classmates something comforting to lean against—a soft, cushiony surface. As for the Yamahas, I always associate pianos with deep feeling, and I do believe that the most powerful writing comes from exploring things we feel passionate about. However, to do so requires a safe environment, and this is where the teacher's art comes in.

If teachers have not been able to draw their students into the creative process—and learning is nothing if not creative, requiring imagination, invention, innovation, and more—then they have failed as teacher-artists. Nor can teachers induce creativity in the learning group by calling attention to it, by exhortation; the absence of self-conscious "creativity" is essential to the success of this kind of teaching. Most important, all teacher-artists develop their own style and express themselves in personal ways. Each person's talent, being unique, pushes him or her in a particular direction. Just as there are no formulas for a particular piece of writing, there are none for a teacher to follow.

I see a parallel here with writing poetry, fiction, or non-fiction. The art aspect doesn't happen at will. It's a by-product of the creator's engagement with her unconscious, informing the work if the writer has gone far enough into her depths.

Consequently, I've never felt there is a hyphen, slash, or any other kind of separation between the words writer(artist)teacher. Trying to separate them seems artificial. If writers are functioning in their artist role, then they inevitably teach. Art challenges our usual ways of thinking and perceiving. Similarly, if teachers are teaching well, they work as artists in the classroom, awakening their students, replacing old structures with new ones, taking up residence in their students' psyches, becoming internalized guides to new levels of awareness.

None of this happens without a risk. Learning writing can stir anxiety in most people. Though Cervantes has said that the pen is the tongue of the mind, that writing springs from the body and is an organic act (in *Finnegans Wake*, James Joyce also says writing is as natural as sweating), current research shows that writing, unlike speech, is not a natural activity. It draws on a different brain function and must be learned. Also, to write well requires peeling away some of the veils we hide behind, another anxiety-producing activity. It can be frightening to be so exposed on the page. A writing teacher, therefore, must be skillful not just in teaching the subject matter, but in managing a classroom, in creating a place where students feel safe to experiment and explore. As I've already suggested, this is where much of the artistry comes in.

Imagination, intuition, and patience are also necessary skills in shaping our own work as writers. We need to listen carefully and follow the writing's lead, not trying too soon to impose order or structure, to assume we know what the material needs. The same thing applies to teaching. I'm reminded of what Axelrod says in *The University Teacher as Artist:* "Every professor of humanities is reliving the Daedalus myth." He emphasizes not only that Daedalus showed Ariadne how the imprisoned Theseus might escape from the labyrinth he designed, but that Daedalus himself was imprisoned in it, along with his son, Icarus. Therefore, in teaching, we are all involved in creating the labyrinth of higher education, sometimes getting lost in it. There is a way out, however. Axelrod says, "The university teacher will not escape the labyrinth by following its passageways. Like Daedalus, he must turn to the artistic imagination. Only as a teacher-artist can the professor make his flight to freedom."

As teachers and writers, we never know for sure what impact our words and personalities will have on our students or readers. Certainly, my former creative writing teacher, M. H., did not know that she came to be a critical, inhibiting presence. If we're lucky, some of our students will let us know if we've gotten through to them in more than a superficial way, if we've stirred something deep that leads to changes in their thinking. The best learning happens when we influence students unconsciously, without them, or us, necessarily being aware of it.

EIGHT

I BELIEVE DREAMS ARE GIFTS FROM MY UNCONSCIOUS THAT give me wonderful (and sometimes not so wonderful) images to live in, the theatre of my sleep. An example is the other night when I awakened from a dream where I was looking at pictures of my first husband's sisters. The whole family was extremely handsome—three boys and six girls. All of them combine French Canadian, some Native Canadian (from the father's side), and Scottish (the mother) ancestry. In the dream, they were now aged and feeling aggrieved by what growing old had done to them, how ugly they'd become. Crones! I was crying in this dream as I talked to someone about how I hated this aspect of growing old, the body's deterioration.

The dream reminds me of one reason I'm seeing an analyst at this phase in my life. It graphically shows how emotional I am about the physical alterations of aging, something I probably wouldn't have been aware of if the dream hadn't brought it to my attention. It's difficult for me to accept how aging physically changes us.

Women suffer the most because of American culture's worship of youth and external beauty. After reaching midlife, many women are discarded, and older women experience the most ageism at their work and in other contexts. How many elderly female TV hosts do you see? Don't most ads that feature older women offer airbrushed images so that aging's deepest cuts don't show up on the face and body? Instead of our skin being a map of our lives, these images camouflage the worst effects through Botox, tucks and lifts, and hair coloring. I've sworn that I'll never do any of these things, and I won't. But not doing them doesn't mean I'm not affected psychologically by our culture's attempts to hide aging's downsides. And my dream illustrates my inner state of mind.

When I left Dr. Y's office today and climbed into my car, I turned on the radio. The station was playing music by a Scottish group from the Isle of Skye where Mum was born, a synchronistic moment. Later, on my walk, I mulled over Dr. Y's question that arose from another dream I'd told him about. He wondered what I could be pushing aside and not wanting to deal with. I envisioned a woman opening a box. And then I thought of Pandora's box and how I don't want everything to come out all at once. But that image made me realize I haven't mourned mum's death fully, even though she moved on in 2007, six days before my birthday.

Once home, I started crying and then sobbing as I remembered that I was her darling, or so she always said. In many ways, we were joined at the hip, and I also share her first name, Lily, though she was known by her middle name, Barbara. No wonder I'm still grieving her death. Maybe engaging with my novel *Fling!* again— which features a ninety-year-old character named Bubbles who strongly resembles my mother—might help me work through more of these feelings.

Mum lived in Calgary, fifteen hundred miles away from my San Francisco Bay area home, and I wasn't with her when she died. Septic shock claimed her after a bladder infection spread to her kidneys, and she was rushed to the hospital. Apparently, the last thing to go is the hearing, so my sister and other family members tried to arouse her through that long night by talking to her.

A few days before, during the last time I'd talked to her on the phone, we were getting ready to hang up, and she'd said, "It's *au revoir* and not goodbye, for parting is such a bitter sigh," a favorite saying of hers. We'd laughed, and I tried not to say goodbye, but I never heard her voice again. I miss her telling me that I mean more to her than anything in the world. I miss her laughter and her singing. I miss her good spirits and determination.

Mum taught me a lot about not being afraid of life, even its bad parts. She didn't avoid illness or death when it hit others or eventually herself. She always tried to visit family or friends who were hospitalized. I also learned to listen to my instincts. To be feisty. To not let people push me around.

Basically, a very open person, Mum was willing to try new things and to embrace differences. Still, at times she displayed her generation's prejudices, freely using the term "I jewed them down." She would have been appalled to realize that her words were hurtful to many people, including my Jewish husband. Her language and behavior were reflexive, not planned.

For all of her faults, and she had many, she loved life. As I've already mentioned, she loved it so much that she lived until 101. I wish she could have lived longer. She was so vital that it's difficult to believe death finally claimed her. Yet in my dreams, she is far from dead. A regular visitor, she continues to age and still is a living presence. Just the other night she showed up yet again in a dream wearing a bikini, not at all uncomfortable with people seeing her aged body. Not trying to cover up her age or who she is, Mum was in full form. In the dream, it did puzzle me that she kept showing up at my California home when I thought she'd returned to Calgary. Who was picking her up and taking her to the airport? Who brought her from the San Francisco airport to my home? A mystery.

The important thing seems to be that she stays close to me, keeping me mindful of the gifts she brought into this world in spite of being abandoned by her mother at fifteen and never seeing her again. It's as if in these dreams she's reassuring me that though she lost her mother early, I'll not lose mine. Ever!

Though I'd returned to Calgary in October 2007 for her memorial service, I wasn't able to be at the early morning interment because my husband and I both caught a stomach flu and didn't sleep much that night. Nor could we be without a toilet. But somehow, I made it to the service later that day and read my eulogy that celebrated Mum and her life. I'll share it with you.

Lily Barbara Gilbertson
Born 6/16/06 — Died 10/14/07

Mum always loved a party, and she would have enjoyed being here with you all. But it's hard to speak of her in the past tense since she's been such a vital figure in my life and in others' as well. She didn't have any advanced degrees, though she admired those who did. Yet she still had an impact on the world just by being "Barbara." She fully embraced life and, in doing so, became a model for others of how to live fully and age well.

Mum came into her own after middle age, discovering in the last part of her life inner resources and strengths that eluded her as a younger woman. Those of you who have already ventured into old age know that "it isn't for sissies." Mum wasn't a sissy. She tackled old age the way she responded on the farm when my stepfather Chester asked her to help him brand and neuter the cattle. She didn't flinch.

Living past 101 is an accomplishment, a major one. Earlier this year, when I told friends I was going to help Mum celebrate her 101st birthday, they expressed disbelief and responded in awe. "101? I can't believe it." But it didn't surprise me.

None of the things I've heard about aging applied to Mum. Most of the time, she slept like a baby. Nor did she discuss the aches and pains that most elderly people complain of, other than being slightly stiff when she got out of a car. And her knees were better than mine. I've had one partial knee replacement and will eventually need a full replacement on the other knee.

Mum was a woman who never made any effort to follow a physical fitness program, whose idea of exercise was to walk from the fridge to the table. She didn't do yoga or any other stretching exercises. And she ate anything and everything: French fries, ice cream, mashed potatoes, gravy, bacon, eggs, chocolates, candies—the works. She didn't hold back with food any more than she did with life.

She did have a religion, though. She loved to shop. I believe shopping kept her vital and enthusiastic about life until she no longer was able to do it on her own, and that wasn't until her late nineties. I don't mean that she was constantly buying items, but it made her feel good to look at colorful clothes and to touch sensuous fabrics, much the same way we might go to an art gallery and admire the artwork. She also loved being out among people. Other humans energized her, and she easily struck up conversations with strangers.

One day, when Mum was eighty-eight, she fell in the bathtub while taking a shower, hitting her head and pulling some muscles, though she claims the fall didn't knock her out. Rather than give in to what had happened, she finished her shower, set her hair, got dressed, put on makeup as usual, and caught the bus about a block away from where she lived. She was heading downtown to her usual shopping haunt, The Bay.

After the trauma of a fall, she needed the reassurance of

her usual routine. She did concede to visit her druggist—not far from the Bay—and bought some Advil, which she took for her headache and other aches and pains. Otherwise, she continued her day as usual.

This reminds me of another fall she'd taken a few years earlier. She'd gone out one winter night—as she did regularly—to play bingo a couple of blocks away. While walking, she hit a patch of ice and her feet went out from under her. I was horrified when she told me about it on the phone the next day. She just cackled and said, "You can't kill an old bird like me."

When Mum turned ninety, my husband and I flew to Calgary from San Francisco for the celebration, joining other family members and friends, a bagpiper, and two young Scottish dancers. We all were there to honor Mum's achievement.

She didn't let us down. When the piper played "Home to the Isles," she stood up, wearing an eye-catching blue lace dress, her pure white hair a halo, and danced back and forth, unable to stop those feet that had trained for highland dancing. And when we invited her, impromptu, to sing a Scottish song herself, she took the microphone like a pro and sang several verses a cappella of "I Ken You're the Laddie That Gave Me the Penny" in a strong, steady voice, not missing a word or a beat.

As Mum aged, she became a talisman for others. Her doctor of many years visited her periodically at home to check up on his prize patient. "I go there to get cheered up."

Everyone wanted to get close to this life force.

At ninety-five, still ambulatory, at the end of her day downtown, Mum went home, refreshed, ready to watch her favorite soap opera, *The Young and the Restless*, before fixing dinner and going out for an evening of bingo. She loved to gamble—bingo and "scratchies." The gambling reflected her attitude on life, her curiosity, her willingness to take a chance. Sometimes she won. Sometimes she lost. More often than not she won.

She was a winner at this game of life, too, though she was realistic enough to know that her days were numbered. But meanwhile, she enjoyed her remaining time.

From watching Mother all these years, I've concluded

that attitude is all. And will. She was a Scot, and she claimed her family's motto was "Do or die." She lived up to this saying. She also adapted to her circumstances, determined to make the best of things wherever she was. She even sang Scottish songs as the orderlies wheeled her into the operating room when she was ninety-five and facing surgery for colon cancer.

Mum loved life so much that she didn't want to let go of it, and those of us who knew her didn't want to see her go. Nancy, a friend of mine who got to know Mum on her many trips to California, said, "I didn't want your mother's life to end. She represented something almost immortal to me!"

Her adventurous spirit, her curiosity, her sense of humor, her lust for life were the keys to Barbara's survival. Wherever she was, she became a presence. When I talked to her on the phone, she loved to say, "They all know Barbara here." And she was right. Wherever she is now, I'm sure they already all know Barbara.

NINE

WHEN I FIRST STARTED WORKING WITH DR. Y, I WAS experiencing a serious bout of insomnia, not a problem I usually have. It had accompanied a sinus infection that overstayed its welcome. Other than minor instances of sleeplessness when going through a traumatic time, insomnia has not been my lifelong companion. The only previous period when I experienced a lingering bout of it was years earlier in 1997. Again, I couldn't sleep because of a chronic sinus infection that lasted for almost a year.

What is it about sinus infections that terrorize me? I tend to get panicky if I can't breathe properly through my nasal passages, especially at night if I awaken with even a slight blockage. I think it's largely connected to fears of dying and not being able to breathe fully. But throughout childhood, I witnessed my stepfather's struggles with asthma. Before the types of medication now available to asthmatics, at times he could barely catch his breath. It was terrifying for me to see this behavior.

The 1997 sinus infection caused severe nasal congestion and made it difficult for me to breathe through my nose. In 2012, it wasn't that severe, but it disturbed me enough that I went to see my internist. He prescribed a dose of oral steroids to reduce the inflammation. Unknown to me then, steroids can inhibit sleep, as they did with me. While they gave me temporary relief from the nasal blockage, it returned when I finished the dosage.

My sleep didn't.

Clearly, sinus infections trigger my death fears. My husband mentioned today that I've often expressed a fear of dying. He's right, and that dread hasn't gone away. Nor do I expect it to. Is there anyone who welcomes death other than those who have a devastating illness and want to be released from it? But I would like to better embrace its reality as part of life. At times I think my fear of death is connected to my fear of the unconscious. I worry that if I open myself fully to that realm, I'll experience terrible things, so at times I push it away.

Yet I'm certain that one way to be free of my fears is to face them, become aware of them through reverie, "active imagination," or whatever way works. (Jung used what he called active imagination to assimilate unconscious contents—dreams, fantasies, etc.—through some form of creative expression: painting, drawing, sculpting, dance.) I know that writing fiction, poetry, or even non-fiction has been a form of active imagination for me at times.

It's possible that the insomnia I experienced had multiple determinants, including a resistance to the inner work I had started doing with Dr. Y. A dream I had then seemed to support this notion: My husband and I were staying at a resort by the sea, and I recall watching the waves rolling in with extreme force. It seemed to be the Atlantic I was looking at, and I thought the water would be too cold for swimming. I saw a number of people fully clothed in order to keep warm and riding what resembled car seats that appeared to be controlled by something holding them all together. The occupants rode on these seats from far out in the sea to shore. Later, I learned that these waters had a severe undertow and even grown men would have trouble fighting it. I warned my son, L (a boy still in the dream), not to go near it.

The ocean often is a symbol for the unconscious, and here I'm keeping my distance from those who were brave enough to enter the waters clothed, suggesting that they had some defense against the elements. It's promising that something is supporting them, but the undertow could be dangerous, and I'm concerned that my younger masculine self—my son—could be in danger if he went too far out. This seems wise—not to venture any further than what I'm comfortable with at the moment.

Another dream showed me moving out of an apartment complex on Meadowsweet Drive that I'd lived in years ago. I knew it would be an emotional departure since so much had happened during the time I'd lived there from the mid to late seventies. I'd recently divorced R, my second husband, and was once again the sole support of my then sixteen-year-old son, born of my first husband. It was a stressful time. I was managing a nineteen-unit apartment complex to support us and also attending college, working on my BA in English with an emphasis on creative writing.

Dr. Y and I talked about what "attitude" I've lived in for so long. I said, "Attitude is too limiting. I inhabited more than one attitude or perspective during those years." It had been a time of much intellectual, psychological, and other growth. I went from being dependent on R, at least emotionally, to being fully independent. I also had begun developing more of an inner life by entering therapy and was increasingly more self-aware. Dr. Y noted that I was leaving a sweet meadow and that this dream seemed to signal where our work together might take me. Am I finally leaving this psychic home I've lived in for so long? If so, it's a major shift.

Before our session was over, I asked Dr. Y what archetypes might form the core of my personality. I believe archetypes express an unconscious complex that has been buried and that can eventually surface. In Jung's view, there are certain motifs that pop up everywhere—in myths, fairy tales, and other world literature, as well as in our fantasies and dreams. We all seem to participate in these themes since they appear in all human life. The mother and father archetype belong to this category, and, in Jung's words, seem "to be part of the inherited structure of the psyche."

Just as seeds we plant in the earth contain preordained structures (that's how dissimilar plants are differentiated), so, too, does each individual. Some of us may be more motherly and fatherly, meaning that we're drawn to having families and playing out these established roles. Others may be artists or follow some other path, though it doesn't mean we can't also be parents. It's just that parenting wouldn't be our primary drive.

I thought the archetype of the girl who can't break free of identifying herself as the "father's daughter" might be my main structure since the *puella aeterna* (eternal girl) is a prominent aspect of my personality. In either case, the girl depends a lot on the father to guide her, often falling victim to a patriarchy and following its lead. But Dr. Y thought I make a better companion to the patriarch than a daughter. He said, "You can tell me if I'm off base, but that's my take on you." He sees me more as a *hetaera* (companion), a female role that has been around since classical Athens and even earlier. It's a mode that felt familiar to me when I'd first read about *hetairas*. Some *hetaera* were high-class prostitutes, but many were part of an elite culture, providing "flattering and skillful conversation,"[7] seen as a significant part of the *hetaira*'s role.

According to Rebecca Futo Kennedy, the term *hetaera* designated "both a status and a set of behaviors . . . There is evidence that the status of *hetaera* designated a woman who could not, for a variety of reasons, contract a formal marriage."[8] These accounts resonate for me, describing the kind of relationships with men I've had over the years. I've always had male friends. Many of these friendships didn't include a sexual or romantic element. I valued being treated as an equal and loved having long conversations with them. Peter Rice-Jones, an artist who is now dead, had been my friend since fifth grade. We kept in touch over the years, and I was one of the last people he wanted to talk to before he died. We did have a brief romantic fling when I was in my early twenties, but we quickly discovered that the strength of our connection was fraternal.

When I did secretarial work in my late teens and early twenties, I found myself hanging out with my bosses, enjoying in-depth conversations, even though at that time my formal education had ended when I dropped out of high school at the end of the tenth grade when I was fourteen. I think Dr. Y has identified me correctly as part of the *hetaera* archetype. I can imagine myself in ancient Greece, overseeing salons and enjoying friendships with men that at times also had a sexual dimension.

In contrast, the father's daughter tends to be a good girl and tries to please her progenitor, constantly elevating him. I've certainly found myself living out this track as well. How could that not happen in a largely patriarchal world? Both *puella* and *hetaira* try to please a man but in different ways. According to Dr. Susan E. Schwartz, a Jungian analyst, "In being father dominated, the Puella woman cannot access the feminine and therefore cannot find who she is."[9] In other words, she is so immersed in the father perspective that she can't see beyond it.

Discerning what archetypes may be influencing me can be a step in separating from them enough to not let them dominate. Knowing that I have this affinity for men helps me to understand why they are such frequent visitors in dreams and, at times, hold so much power over me. Now I can step back and ask myself if I'm being caught in either a *puella* or *hetaera* net that could prevent me from having a more authentic experience—authentic in the sense that I can step out from behind these positions and be more conscious of my deeper desires and needs.

TEN

BEING MARRIED TO SOMEONE WHO SEES HIMSELF, IN PART, AS a secular intellectual and agnostic, I sometimes feel constrained in how much of my spiritual leanings I show M, though I don't try to hide this part of myself. Whenever possible, I meditate, do yoga, and practice tai chi. I also believe in a divinity. But for me, the Hebrew and Christian God—even though Mary gave birth to Jesus and has a major role in that religion—is too male and therefore too limited in its perspective. The other world religions (all patriarchal) also seem too identified with the masculine view. For me, the word "divinity" feels more generic and not gender bound—an entity that transcends but also participates in our earthly lives.

However, I love myths and reading about the various gods and goddesses because I feel they reveal something essential about humans. The Greek pantheon is rich in deities who seem to be part of our psychological lives. Mars represents the aggressive energy that can lead to wars. Aphrodite offers the opposite as a love figure. Athena demonstrates that females can blend both masculine and feminine qualities and also be leaders. And the list goes on.

My husband knows of my Jungian orientation and thoroughly supports my analysis with Dr. Y. Though M and I have different paths, we share many similar values and interests. He can read my Magritte piece (included in Chapter 5) and fully affirm its insights. I can support his psychoanalytic work and appreciate the ways in which he's helping his patients lead better, less conflicted, deeper lives.

For the past few days, I've been reviewing the early months of my work with Dr. Y and exploring what I've discovered so far. One of our first sessions began with the dream image of women creating an arch with their legs for me to pass through. As I've already said, Dr. Y had noted it resembled a birth passage. His observation suggests that our time together could inaugurate a new phase for me. This idea of new life was reinforced when I dreamt of a baby that needed my attention in the night. The child was crying, keeping me awake, as was other activity happening in the rooms around me.

Babies, totally reliant on their parents, need us to respond to their physical needs and their desires. In this case, whatever has been born in me will keep me awake if necessary in order to be heard. The same seems to be true for whatever other activity that's happening in the surrounding rooms. Something has been awakened. Whatever it is wants me to know that having this new life requires a commitment similar to one I'd make if I actually had a baby to care for.

When we give birth to an actual child, we see the external and internal worlds with fresh eyes through this new life. In old age, I appear to be taking on the unexpected responsibility of giving birth to myself in ways I hadn't expected. As long as we're alive, we're evolving. But like any endeavor, raising this inner child will involve commitment, just as being a writer does. Yet this pledge unravels regularly, daily even, just as happens in any other relationship. We must constantly recommit ourselves. I like what Erica Helm Meade says about commitment in her book *Tell It by Heart*:

> I recalled the good things which had come to me as a result of my commitment to tend the garden [i.e., life as a garden bursting with possibility], and I realized what Goethe meant in saying that when one commits oneself, providence moves too, and help arrives from inexplicable sources.... I realized all the riches in my life—the love and creativity—had blossomed from commitment—from my ability to hang in and persist, even when I couldn't remember why. The vow to the muse was like marriage: When the passion wanes, commitment sustains us until the juice comes flooding back.

Or as the *I Ching* claims, "Persistence furthers."

I suspect there might be many more possibilities of renewals in store for me, depending on how long I live. Old age doesn't mean we stop growing and learning. While we do contract in certain ways and give up some functions, we also make gains, all of which require attentiveness to our inner processes—to ourselves. The gains often involve deeper insights into who we are and the passing scene, our inner and outer worlds.

In many of my dreams, some kind of separation has been happening. Could this theme suggest that I'm detaching myself from aspects of my younger self as I'm giving birth to newer versions? It seems to me that this kind of separating and reconnecting is an important part of any growth process. Often, we must detach ourselves from a perspective or an attitude that is no longer fruitful before we can move on to one that better fits our changing and expanding outlook. As a result, these separations from aspects of my younger self seem important. They free me to find a new, deeper way of living with it.

But what in my younger self do I need to revise? I'm thinking of my attitude toward aging, my notion that it will be all downhill. I hope to grow into a more expansive notion of what my aging self could be. I'm thinking of a woman I know who is in her mideighties, but you'd never know it given her energy and focus. I had a conversation with her recently in an email where she pointed out that eighty is just a number. For her, "Time just seems to go on, and we weather the storms as they come."

I love the way she views time. It does seem to go on unless we get hung up in monitoring it too closely. When I do this, I try to control it. But it isn't controllable. If we avoid dominating it, we're likely to age more easily, and that may be one of the things I'm revising just now, the need to cling so tightly to time rather than letting it run its course, which it will anyway.

Speaking of revising, I've been reviewing my novel *Freefall: A Divine Comedy*, a work that features Tillie Bloom, an installation artist. I share her concerns about how difficult it is to discern what we mean by matriarchies and patriarchies, as well as masculine and feminine, since there are so many meanings to each term. These could be other perspectives that I need to update rather than cling to my outdated ideas. Still, one thing that doesn't need much updating is the reality, which most people accept, that we live in a patriarchal culture where the male point of view dominates to such a degree that it can be difficult to tease out what female qualities might look like. For those of us who grew up viewing ourselves through these male lenses, how can we ever connect fully with the sources of our being? How can we more completely know our female selves?

Before the pandemic, while I was sitting on an exercise bike at a gym I'd attended for several years, I looked around and realized what a masculine space it is. All of the TV screens featured a male sport activity, and the place has a square, spare look that I associate with males—strange since more than half the membership is female. This recognition made me pause.

Of course, I know that I inhabit a male-dominated world. But we women, especially those my age, have accommodated ourselves so well to masculinized spaces that we hardly realize it any longer. Without questioning our surroundings, we take for granted that men have most of the power whether in the workplace or even in the home. Since most architects are male (even today, only seventeen percent are women), they are responsible for designing our public spaces.

This moment in the gym stayed with me and caused me to look more closely at my environs, trying to discern what they reveal about our culture and women's place within it. So I wasn't surprised when a recent article in *The New York Times* pointed out that the dummies used for simulating car crashes are created from male measurements, and the car manufacturers don't take into account women's physical differences. Therefore, vehicles' built-in safety features don't protect female drivers or passengers as much as they do males.

In many of the dreams and conversations I had with Dr. Y in the early months of our work together, one dominating theme was that of men being in control. In these dreams, I often feel as if I don't have enough substance or wherewithal or financial resources and need a man who has more. My relationship with my husband is a good example of how I've lived out this dynamic. During our early years together, I let him take the lead when we had dinner with friends. He was so much better at expressing himself that I hid behind my writer's persona, observing the dynamics at play between everyone, making mental notes, and keeping my input to a minimum. This approach allowed me to conceal what I considered my inadequacies. I feared I couldn't equal M intellectually. Now that I'm less fearful of speaking out, I'm stepping forward more and not being such a wallflower.

These sessions with Dr. Y are like collaborating with another artist. Material that seems mundane and at times incomprehensible becomes transformed. Themes I hadn't noticed when recording or reviewing my dreams on my own become apparent. The dialogue between inner and outer worlds sharpens. It's as if in those forty-five minutes each week, we enter one large dream, and I'm highly conscious of being in the analytic container. The pressure on that vessel magnifies the work, illuminates it, crystallizes it.

I also find that my emotions can erupt unexpectedly at those times, showing me the power of something I wouldn't have noticed if I weren't engaged in our weekly dialogue. This response happens less easily on my own. Somehow, I'm more vulnerable in these one-on-one meetings. It's as if I undress psychologically before entering, leaving fewer ways to hide. As they say, it all hangs out. I hang out.

Another thing I'm conscious of in our sessions is a mysterious presence. As it says in Scripture: "For where two or three gather in my name, there am I with them." (Matt. 18:20 NIV) In Jungian parlance, that "I" would be the "Self." Jung believed the Self might equally be called the "God within us," and dreams are a major way we access this entity. I think something profound can occur between two people who are trying to meet at a deeper level, whose intention is to engage the Self, a part of my psyche that knows more about me than my conscious ego does.

ELEVEN

I'M NOT SURE WHEN THE CHANGE HAPPENED. IT COULD HAVE been fifty years ago when I dove into a deep depression that lasted for a year. Lost in the unconscious, I seemed to have misplaced myself, or at least the self I had been familiar with until that time: the high-school dropout who had become a single parent because something in her wanted more from life than what her first husband offered; the party girl; the young woman who had married R, her second husband, a man she didn't trust but who needed his emotional support.

In those early years, I frequently turned to my older sister for guidance and support. She was a committed Christian and thought I was undergoing a conversion process—my old self was dying so I could be reborn in Christ. Convinced she was right, I went to the Lutheran church down the street from where I lived because R, my husband at that time, was a Lutheran. The minister not only baptized me but also my ten-year-old son, though before the baptism, the pastor wanted to have a conversation with me. We met in his office, and he's the one who encouraged me to meet with the Reverend Elmer Laursen, the psychologist I mentioned in an earlier section that helped me through my deep depression.

Those weekly visits opened doors into my interior that had been locked for twenty-seven years. Laursen was the kind of fatherly figure I'd lacked growing up. He sat across from me in his short-sleeved black chaplain uniform, a white clerical collar circling his neck, and let me talk and emote. The gap between his front teeth, and the boyish smile that radiated his face, contrasted with his thinning white hair. Perhaps his link to God made me more open with him, the idea that this man channeled a superpower who could forgive me for whatever sins I felt I had committed. Neither of us was Catholic, but the dynamic definitely was confessional, and I can see its value. He mainly listened, occasionally asking me questions, making observations at times. Opening up in this way offered me a release valve for some of what I had repressed over the years. Slowly, I found keys that opened locked doors and began to work my way out of the black sludge that engulfed me.

Laursen not only was my confessor, but he also stirred my intellect. I wanted to read more about Christianity, a religion I'd paid lip service to during my childhood. I'd reluctantly attended Sunday school classes at Mum's occasional urging, though she wasn't a regular churchgoer. Nor was my stepdad. They made their twice-yearly church appearances at Christmas and Easter.

Sunday school actually had turned me off Jesus, the man I was supposed to love and who apparently loved me in return. I didn't know then what love meant, but it seemed demanding, and I didn't feel up to it. Nor did I admire Jesus. My Sunday school teachers posted his glossy pictures on the classroom walls, and they always presented him as a kind of limp-wristed, tanned, longhaired guy with a syrupy smile who carried a white shepherd's crook. How could I love him?

The good news is that my parents gave up their idea that I needed religion and let me run wild. They weren't attentive parents; other things preoccupied them. My mother was having an affair with our French-Canadian boarder. He lived with us for several years before my stepdad wised up and kicked him out. And my stepdad, who worked at a rock crushing plant as a laborer, was too exhausted to pay much attention to me or anything else.

So how did I at twenty-seven decide that Christianity had something to tell me? How could it help me live my life? Pastor Laursen became my model of a reasonable and accepting Christian that I found credible. He recognized my thirst for knowledge and began loaning me books by various theologians and other religious writers. Paul Tillich's *The Courage to Be* was particularly helpful for me since I was very anxious, and Tillich put anxiety within a helpful religious context. And there were other writers whose names I now forget. But John Sanford's *Dreams: Gods Forgotten Language* stayed with me. Sanford had worked as a parish priest for nineteen years. In 1974, he left the church for full-time work as a Jungian analyst and psychotherapist, lecturing and authoring a series of books. They took me to places that still resonate, especially the role dreams have in mediating our inner and outer worlds. I was moved, and I began to investigate Carl Jung's ideas more systematically.

At that point, I hadn't given up organized religion. I was still a neophyte, trying to find my way in this new territory, and I also thought I might still find salvation in the protestant church. I even ended up working in a couple of churches, enough time to teach me that while organized religious observance can be valuable for some people, it wasn't for me. Churchianity seemed a better word for what I was experiencing. I decided that if someone named Jesus had ever roamed this earth and now returned to discover this religion in his name, he would be horrified. It represented many of the things he preached against—spiritual pride, greed, hypocrisy, indifference to human need, and unbelief.

My later work in two presbyterian churches showed me the constraints of the established Christian church's hierarchy. It also made me feel boxed in and trapped by the male-dominated institution. My time there doing administrative work gave me a perspective on the pastors—male and female—that undermined my ability to see them as true links to anything holy. All the ones I knew—one female and three males—were sexually involved with church members. In the female's case, she had a husband and two sons and was coming out as a lesbian. She ended up having affairs with several women in the congregation before settling on one whose marriage also splintered. The male pastors were all married but carrying on with multiple females who were drawn to their God-like authority and power.

I wasn't naive, but it seemed that human foibles and imperfections stood out even more in this setting. The male and female spiritual leaders may have been well intentioned when they started out, and certainly not all individuals who work for religious institutions get corrupted by the power of being God's earthly representatives. Yet it happens frequently enough to make one realize how vulnerable we all are to such forces. Of course, this was before recent reports of the many individuals who, as children, have been sexually abused by church officials.

When I was seeing Dr. Laursen, even though I hadn't earned my GED yet, I always had been an avid reader and was eager to learn more about the current path I was on. Laursen's library was a great resource for me, the beginning of a lifelong quest for knowledge of not only the inner world but also the outer one. I wanted to be like Socrates and know myself as well as others. I wanted to live in an enlarged consciousness that included my nightly dreams as well as my daytime fantasies.

So while I had trouble "worshipping" in any traditional, institutional manner, I felt a deep recognition of and connection to something ineffable. This was my first step in communing with my inner world and discovering that such a thing even existed. When I read about the unconscious at that time, I had no idea what it was until it "claimed" me. This was the beginning of my attempts to find and retrieve a deeper self, leading to my eventually working with Jungian-trained therapists and analysts who understood my spiritual yearnings as well as my psychological needs. While I didn't find "God," the patriarchal white entity at the head of most Christian churches, I did discover the divine.

I no longer expect to find the ineffable in so-called religious institutions. Instead, museums that feature the world's great artists have become my link to whatever mysteries the universe contains. I've visited many of them during travels my husband and I have taken, including one of the greatest, St. Petersburg's Hermitage Museum. Artists may not be promoting a particular god or goddess, or even a spiritual dimension, but that's exactly why museums appeal to me. They don't offer dogma. Instead, artists invite us to join them in their explorations of the world we inhabit and let us discover whatever truth their art may be expressing. I had lost religion but found the divine.

TWELVE

NOT LONG AGO, I REREAD AN ESSAY BY CAROL CHRIST, AN academic who is the eleventh chancellor of the University of California, Berkeley, the first woman to hold that post. In "The New Feminist Theology: A Review of the Literature," Christ discusses how women need their own divinity to worship. I recall reading the essay in the 1970s, not long after it was published, along with Mary Daly's *Beyond God the Father*. Even then, I was searching for a divinity different from what the mainly male-dominated traditions had passed down.

I also was aware of the feminist theorist Starhawk, who in 1979 published *The Spiral Dance: A Rebirth of the Ancient Religion of the Great Goddess*. It has become a classic text on Wicca, modern witchcraft, spiritual feminism, feminist neopaganism, ecofeminism, and the Goddess movement, which is a mouthful! What do all of these terms mean? I won't try to answer that question since Starhawk does her best to do so in the book.

But when *The Spiral Dance* was released, I rejected it because the contents seemed flaky to me then. I think it's one reason I didn't get caught up in the goddess thing at that time and continue to reject it for the most part. Even though I'm a feminist in the sense that I seek social justice and equality for everyone, no matter his or her gender, I also think a part of me resists the idea of losing a male god and his authority. I'm sure that response comes from growing up in a household where males were in charge and also from living in a culture that has mirrored what I experienced at home. It's hard to escape early training. That's another reason why I prefer a genderless divinity.

However, in rereading Starhawk today, I'm surprised at how much sense she makes, though I still resist many of the terms she uses, especially "witch" since it has so many negative connotations. However, I'm okay with "pagan" and have often said I prefer the pagan approach that preceded the Judeo-Christian religions. My understanding is that before monotheism, many of our ancestors recognized multiple deities, male and female, yet I've recently learned that the term paganism wasn't associated with those who lived then. According to Glen Warren Bowersock, author of *Late Antiquity: A Guide to the Postclassical World*:

> The adoption of *paganus* by the Latin Christians as an all-embracing, pejorative term for polytheists represents an unforeseen and singularly long-lasting victory, within a religious group, of a word of Latin slang originally devoid of religious meaning. The evolution occurred only in the Latin west, and in connection with the Latin church. Elsewhere, "Hellene" or "gentile" *(ethnikos)* remained the word for "pagan"; and *paganos* continued as a purely secular term, with overtones of the inferior and the commonplace.

Nor did "paganism" have formalized rituals or an organized system of beliefs. During my quest in the 1970s, I wanted to recover a time when the main religions hadn't yet dominated western and eastern cultures. I sought an individual experience of the Divine, a personal gnosis and interaction with something beyond our limited earthly knowledge.

As for Starhawk, I still don't want to be identified with a movement so far out of the mainstream. It reminds me of a recent dinner party my husband and I attended. A couple we had just met sat across from us in the dining room. We were in the midst of a lively discussion over bowls of gelato sprinkled with pomegranate seeds when they mentioned they were Christian Scientists. We and the other two diners avoided each other's eyes, gliding around this announcement, trying to digest what we'd heard. All professionals, we'd never dined before with a Christian Scientist—that we were aware of. The movement seems like something from another planet, especially if viewed from our intellectual and cultural sphere. And yet, there they were, perfectly "normal" people who were following a sect that believes prayer can cure disease.

My difficulty with their stance illuminates why I've had trouble embracing Wicca. While I love some fringe ideas, including some aspects of the occult, such as *The Tarot*, I also respect clear thinking. I believe most of my friends share this perspective, so even at my age, I don't want to be identified with the kind of esoteric beliefs that Starhawk represents. For all of its faults, the patriarchy still embodies many positive attributes, including some facets of rationality and scholarship. But, of course, that could also be one of its main problems. Such rationality and scholarship could prevent me and others from seeing something other, and that other might be a perspective closer to a more female way of being in the world.

While I was doing all my recent goddess reading, I had the following dream that I shared with Dr. Y: I had my son, L, drive me to an out of the way place in nature. The road was one lane, and I wondered if I should be driving because I felt more confident negotiating the primitive trails in that area than L did. But we reached our destination safely. The house seemed to be owned by a woman I knew in the dream and whose guest I was, though I don't think I'd mentioned to her that L would join me for part of the time. Meanwhile, L and I would have the place to ourselves until she arrived. It was a huge house with many bedrooms in an isolated area. When L and I first went inside, we found that wild animals had taken up residence there, including a pretty tame lion that I tried to avoid. I was grateful it didn't pay any attention to me. I guess a door had been left open, allowing these creatures to find their way inside, but we managed to redirect them. At one point, L had invited a friend to come see this mansion, but I felt uneasy about him being there should the owner turn up. He didn't stay long. I also was uncomfortable about L being there because I hadn't mentioned to the owner that he would be joining me. I wondered if I would need to pay something for his board and room. Mine, I guess, was free.

After I recorded this dream, I wondered if it had anything to do with the Starhawk book I was reading before I fell asleep since her rituals and beliefs are strongly rooted in nature, a sacred entity for her. The dream narrative reminds me of a fairy tale where the children go deep into a forest where a witch lives. Could reading about witches and Wicca in *The Spiral Dance* contribute to me dreaming of seeking this place in nature? And who is this woman whose house I'm using? Clearly, to own this manor, she must have means, and such means can equate with power. Could the woman who owns this place be connected to Starhawk or some equivalent, someone who has created her own structure that she tries to anchor in nature?

It also seems to be a place where not only masculine and feminine can merge, but wild beasts also can live. As Dr. Y noted, animals are impinging on this civilized dwelling. Since the female owner has left a door open, she must have realized that wild animals could easily find refuge in her house. They seemed to take for granted that it was okay to be in this place that is just another part of the natural world. Dr. Y wondered if one of the differences between this nature-based spirituality and the more traditional way has something to do with culture being over and against nature. Currently, in most places in the world, civilization is in conflict with nature. Perhaps the dream is showing a different approach: culture and nature need to be integrated so there's less splitting. Dr. Y thought that might be one difference between a more traditional masculine approach and what someone like Starhawk is advocating.

When I reflected more on the dream, I was intrigued with the idea that I'm bringing this masculine figure, my son, into this female space, though I don't have the owner's permission. And he's so impressed with having access to her estate that he wants to share it with his male friends. It makes me wonder if this reaction from the masculine side of my personality doesn't show that the two worlds can blend. It doesn't have to be either/or.

Given that I'm trying to learn more about what goddess worship involves, this dream suggests I don't mind spending time in this female's mansion. It's okay to get to know her and have a relationship with her. If I apply this dream narrative to what I'm taking away from *The Spiral Dance*, I believe that what Starhawk and her associates are doing has value. I admire her attempts to embrace multiple perspectives and to promote the idea of there not being just a single goddess or god functioning independently. Instead, she believes these two realms must work together, live together.

I believe hierarchies, though necessary at times, can be dangerous because they can get out of hand. To counter those dangers, Starhawk and others in the Wiccan world have stopped using terms such as "high priestess," employing the word leader instead, leaving behind the mystifying language. Of course, they may be deluding themselves. We may not call ourselves by a name that suggests special status, but it doesn't prevent us from thinking we should be treated differently. The power drive has a way of creeping into even these institutions and the individuals who act as leaders.

Starhawk has discarded her given name and chosen one that certainly is distinctive. It suggests that she herself is a kind of star—whether of the Hollywood or celestial type, I don't know—and a hawk, again an elevated designation. But I believe her main message is inclusiveness where "the goddess" is an all-encompassing being, Gaia the shared common mother of all species. Yet with most Edens, there also is a snake lurking somewhere, ready to undermine these idealistic notions.

As for what all of this means for me internally, personally, I'm not hungering for a god or a goddess to worship. I feel I'm already connected to some kind of transcendence that is more or less ineffable. But I'm happy to have revisited my earlier resistance to the Starhawk world and reviewed my prejudices. I still have them, yet I hope they've softened somewhat.

Dr. Y has pointed out that in the past, I've taken a conventional religious path in seeking spiritual answers, which is true. In my early years as a seeker, I attended services and bible studies in various protestant churches, checking out the differences between Episcopal and Presbyterian, Methodist and United Church offerings. Some of what I discovered in these institutions comes through in the interlinked short stories of my yet-to-be published work *The Sinner's Club*. Dr. Y believes I'm on my own path, seeking what Jung calls individuation, a process by which individuals can become more authentically what they are as opposed to what they "should be." Dr. Y wonders if I'm talking about my own individuation process in these sessions with him.

He went on to point out that because of my reading this material on goddesses, part of what I'm saying is "I know I'm not that." People realize their identity from the time they're toddlers by saying "no," which is what I've been doing. Though I'm no longer a toddler, I'm still going through a similar process of carving out who I am by identifying what I'm not.

It's also causing me to consider more carefully what these words masculine and feminine mean. If I explore a more feminine doctrine, I still need to distinguish between true and false perspectives just as I would in a more masculine approach. But then again, is it even possible to separate these two distinctive-but-merged ways of being in the world? And why should we unless it's to determine when one or the other perspective becomes too dominant and misuses its power.

I think we're all limited in our knowledge of whatever else exists in the universe we inhabit. We're like ants in terms of the vastness of what's out there or inside us compared to what we know of it, limited in our vision and understanding. I do believe there is an afterlife of some kind, but I don't think we have the capacity in our current earthly state to understand what it might be like. Our ideas seem so simplistic, as with reincarnation. If we do have contact with one another after death, I'm sure it's an experience we can't comprehend with our limited earthly selves because what comes after is unfathomable. Otherwise, there would be no mystery.

What's the point in visiting a foreign country if we know ahead of time what we'll experience? When we visit a foreign country, and I'm thinking here of one that is truly different in terms of language and values, we might read about it beforehand and see travelogues, but nothing replaces our direct involvement of being there in person. Planning for such a trip—as happened for us when we have visited distinctly different places such as Greece, Turkey, Morocco, and Russia—fills us with both fear and excitement because we're entering an unknown. But those two emotions are part of creating the mystery that makes travel itself so rewarding. I hope I can take that feeling with me as I near the end of my temporal life and am approaching a very different kind of journey. But, of course, I am reaching the end of my life. Yet it's still difficult to view myself as being at that stage.

Helen Luke, a Jungian analyst, in her book *Old Age: Journey into Simplicity*, also sees aging as a mystery, just as Shakespeare did. She quotes a few of King Lear's words that she believes are the climax of his whole speech, and goes on to comment on them:

> "And take upon us the mystery of things, as if we were God's spies." This is the final responsibility of each person's life. Will we or will we not, as we approach the prison of old age, accept this supreme task? . . . To them comes the great opportunity of taking upon themselves the mystery of things, of becoming, as it were, God's spies. A spy is one who penetrates into a hidden mystery, and a spy of God is that one who sees at the heart of every manifestation of life, even behind the trivial talk of "poor rogues," the *mysterium tremendum* that is God . . . The true mystery is the eternal paradox at the root of life itself—it is that which, instead of hiding truth, reveals the whole, not the part.

The mystery is what draws me onward, the desire to pull closer to it and, perhaps, become "a spy of God." It's the time of life when we can honor our deepest natures and still make astonishing findings about ourselves.

THIRTEEN

D URING TODAY'S SESSION WITH DR. Y, I TOLD HIM OF A
dream during which I was in a very large apartment complex
across the street from a major construction site that regularly did
things that shook the earth nearby. While people who lived in the
place didn't seem worried about the quaking that was damaging
the building, it was clear to me that an old structure like that was
going to feel the impact and could eventually collapse. To prove my
point, a huge crossbeam fell. Luckily, no one was injured, but it did
suggest I was right.

This dream implies that the apartment complex has to go. Of
course, complex has multiple meanings. It's also a psychoanalytical
term that describes "a related group of emotionally significant ideas
that are completely or partly repressed and that cause psychic conflict,
leading to abnormal mental states or behavior."[10] Could this be the
disintegration of a psychological complex that is too old and needs
to be rebuilt from better material to withstand what's coming? Will
the construction that's going on lead to a sturdier center for old age?
That really is my goal from this process: to find a better stance in
relationship to aging so I don't feel so shaken by whatever comes up.
That is my destination. The dream fits with others I've brought to our
sessions that show corresponding movement in my psyche—renewal.

I also brought a dream to this session that included Dr. Y. He
ended up in the front seat of our car, sitting between M and me. M
was driving, and we seemed to be giving Dr. Y a lift somewhere.
However, the M who was driving did not look at all like my husband.
He had a round face and resembled an Irishman (apt for a James
Joyce scholar!). He introduced himself to Dr. Y and commented on
his wife's treatment. Dr. Y told him there was movement, but we all

seemed unsure of how to reach our destination, and a GPS wouldn't be much help. I felt impatient and said, "We can still read a map. We aren't helpless." From my perspective, we can find our way. Maps give us guidelines and offer clues to where we are. An overview. While they may not take us directly to our destination as a GPS does, they can point us in the right direction.

The dream appeared to be showing that Dr. Y could intercede between the me/my ego and the particular male attitude that M—the male who is driving—represents in this dream. Dr. Y could be mediating the secular M in my psyche with my non-secular self. Since M is driving in this instance and not me, I'm relying on him to steer the psychic vehicle I get around in. Still, there seems an easy flow between us all in the front seat. No one is in the back. But I do wonder why M is driving this vehicle and not me. Is the dream showing that this male perspective is in the driver's seat? If so, what effect might he have in squelching my pursuit of more irrational ideas? It's something I need to watch out for in myself. Do I give too much latitude to this inner M?

Or is the dream showing me that I don't always have to be in the driver's seat? I can be a passenger and trust that this male who is driving can assist in following whatever directions I give him from the map I'm using.

The main theme of today's dreams was movement. Dr. Y got a better sense of M—he's Jewish, he teaches, and is a Joyce scholar; thoughts come easily to him. Dr. Y said that for those whose feeling function from Jung's psychological types predominates, which is the case for me, it takes longer to think, hence writing is an easier mode of communication for me because I have time to gather my thoughts.

Dr. Y believes I'm giving birth to myself at a deeper level. He also thinks I'm making a descent into the underworld. He said, "Not that you should make or have to make a descent, but you are making it, even if you don't really know what it's about yet."

FOURTEEN

It was strange to visit the Crescent Confectionary last night in a dream. When I was thirteen, I went with Chester, my stepdad, to the Confectionary, and he asked Mr. Larson, the owner, to give me a part-time job. Chester bought most of our food there on credit, paying the bill when he was flush. A toothless Mr. Larson looked me over and said he'd try me out.

Drool gathered in the creases of his wizened face and dripped off his chin. Both Mr. Larson and his daughter Bert wore deeply soiled aprons, grime filled every seam in their hands, tobacco stains had turned their index fingers brown, and Bert's hair seemed to have been washed in oil. They often worked with a cigarette dangling from the corner of their mouths, ashes falling into grocery bags and produce.

But in my dream, the place was now a classy restaurant, lit from within by dimmed, low-hanging pendant lights and candles, having gone through a major revision under new owners. I was standing outside, staring through a large window. A couple sat at a table next to it, eating. It seemed strange to be standing outside, looking into this vastly changed space where I'd once worked.

From the shadows, an unfamiliar woman appeared. I turned to her and said, "I dream frequently of this place."

She said, "I dream of it, too, at least six times a year."

I was surprised to hear that someone else had been impacted by the store. When I worked there, it was a confectionary, but sweets were a minor item, not featured. It had a soda fountain where we made milkshakes, sundaes, banana splits, and floats, but groceries, toys, clothes, magazines, and cosmetics also crammed the two rooms.

I partially came of age there. It was my first official job other than babysitting. Mr. Larson paid me 35¢ an hour, an amount that seemed huge at the time—the early 1950s. I had to wait on a variety of people, serving them at the counter. I also had to lug wooden crates of soft drinks from the basement upstairs, as well as boxes of canned goods, shelving them and dusting the rest.

Chester actually ended up paying my salary, though he didn't realize it. Whenever he made a purchase, either Mr. Larson or Bert wrote down each thing in cramped handwriting on the stained sheets of a ruled notebook. The paper curled at the edges and the ink ran. There was no cash register tape to itemize each purchase. It was all based on trust, but I knew from watching Bert and Mr. Larson that they weren't trustworthy. I had seen them put a little extra weight on the scale when they were weighing sliced sandwich meat— bologna, spiced ham, salami. Nothing prevented them from padding the monthly bill they gave my stepdad, and he never questioned the charges, grateful they let him buy things when he didn't have the cash up front.

A crescent signifies an early stage in the moon's monthly evolution, representing the moon in an early period. I associate the moon and its images with the feminine principle. When I worked at the Confectionery, I also was at an early stage in my life, beginning to feel my female self take root but still having many other phases ahead of me. Just as the crescent moon is limited in what it can illuminate, so too was I restricted at that time. I not only didn't know what my future had in store for me, I also didn't appear to have a future. Chester didn't think girls needed to be educated. College certainly wasn't a consideration for me. I could have worked at the Confectionery well into adulthood and beyond, or held a similar dead-end job. I didn't, or rather, I couldn't have foreseen a future then that included college and many other triumphs.

In the dream, I cried when I told the shadowy fellow dreamer that I'd lived just a couple of blocks away from the store at 722–4A Street NE, my old neighborhood. That place where I spent my formative years still carries a lot of emotion for me, as does the Confectionery, where I first ventured into the working world. After leaving the farm because of his severe asthma and spending a year living at a rundown hotel in the east end of Calgary, Chester had bought a house in that part of town. Our first real home in the city, the house had been new when we moved into it. We got to know all of our neighbors on 4A Street and surrounding blocks. We kids played at the nearby park, and I made many new friends. No wonder the woman in the dream visits the Confectionary at least six times a year, needing to feel connected still to that stage in both of our lives since she represents some part of myself.

And now, like me, the Confectionary has been transformed. Or maybe its transformation signals that something in me that functioned at a more primary, scattered level, offering a grab bag of goods, has finally found a focus. A restaurant now, it can nourish those who enter its doors, sending them back into the world refreshed and renewed. The early 1950s live on in me and in the store, but both have metamorphosized.

FIFTEEN

L AST SUMMER, A SWARM OF BEES MADE THEIR HOME BETWEEN the outer and inner walls of our house. Through a hole the diameter of a pencil they traveled, the entrance rarely vacant. While one bee balanced on the edge of the hole, preparing for takeoff, others circled and dove, waiting for their chance to enter. With the hive located next to the garden hose, I had to time my passing so I didn't get caught in the bees' flight path, unable to fully relax while working in the yard.

Of course, I had the power to wipe them out at any time. And I was tempted, especially when I watered: all I had to do was focus the hose full force on the entrance to their hive and the bees would be goners.

However, since they also had invaded my dreams, I didn't think I could get rid of them so easily. And as much as I wanted them gone, I didn't want to interfere with their cycle of gathering food and pollinating flowers. I would wait until winter before I acted.

Meanwhile the dreams continued.

In one, the bees had finally entered my house and I was racing from room to room, trying to evade them. I did manage to shut myself in a bedroom, temporarily safe from attack. In another dream, a bee with most of its body gone still had the strength to dive at me. I swiped at it hard, but the bee survived.

Then there was the dream where I was at a Mardi Gras-like event. A young woman who was a former student of mine in waking life, part Indian herself, created an Indian costume in the dream for me to wear, as well as a crown. After wandering around alone for a while, I returned to where I'd left the student, aware of a bee circling my head. I tried to swat it away, but it was persistent. I think the arrangement of my hair around the crown suggested a nest. Hoping the bee would be discouraged, I pulled off the crown and threw it away.

During this time, I also began writing a story inspired by something a neighbor had told me: hundreds of bees had invaded her attic and the exterminators had to be called. I was intrigued by what the situation suggested, curious to pursue the symbolic meaning of the invasion. However, it wasn't until I began to write dialogue for the story that I realized how much of my own inner life was being revealed as I created the characters.

The story unfolded, revealing that numerous boxes were stored in the attic, many of them belonging to the wife, part of an inheritance from her mother and grandmother. A steamer trunk contained family photos, women's gowns from the nineteenth century, and other treasures. Also in the boxes were diaries the woman had kept as a child, paints, ballet slippers, and so on. While she hadn't opened these containers since her marriage, nervous about entering the attic, she did value what was there. Not so her husband, who poked fun at her for hanging onto the things he said were attracting the bees.

Curiously, it wasn't until I came to the end of my bee dream cycle that it dawned on me what was happening with the story. It was articulating my own inner process—the traditional male was denigrating the feminine treasures. The woman's husband was actually right: the boxes—stored away for many years and symbolically representing the woman's creative energy—were attracting the bees.

This reminded me of the dream during which I was wearing the crown, for, after all, I am like this woman. I'm the one who has a feminine inheritance that hasn't been valued or integrated into the main part of the house—it remains in the attic. Rather than wearing something as attention-getting as a crown, which attracted the bees, I took it off, threw it away. That was my solution.

All of this makes me wonder how often in waking life I do the same thing, deny my "royalty"—some quality recognized by the younger female student who has an Indian heritage—royal not in the traditional, aristocratic, elite sense, but in what is valuable, what carries value, wealth, and richness—earthiness.

Later, when I looked at the sheet of paper I had used for clustering associations around the word "bee" in preparation for writing this passage, I was startled by what had happened. While most of the associations were scattered around the page, like bees in flight, there were two columns of single words next to each other. In one column I had noted: dreams, determined, dangerous, afraid, hiding, sting, keep away. In the other were gods, myth, mystery, fantasy, musing, goddesses, eyes.

These words sum up the discoveries I've made about the bees and their relation to my inner world. I was afraid of what they evoked, recalling that as a child on the farm—a time when I had a vivid fantasy life, was entranced by fairy tales and all they suggested, and even possessed a closet inhabited by a whole kingdom, including a king and queen!—we had a beehive in the barn. Not only did we eat the honey the bees made, but I also watched the activity around the honeycombs with considerable curiosity. The bees hummed and sang, crawling all over each other, totally focused on making honey. I was intrigued by the geometric patterns of the individual cells and the amazing transformation happening in front of me. My young eyes were absorbing this mysterious process.

But I soon repressed this impulse to see so deeply. The childhood closet into which I had projected my teeming mythic imagination was cleared out. Into it went practical items; it became simply storage space. So instead of valuing my heritage, the feminine realm that I associate with the imagination, I distrusted it, found it dangerous, kept it at a distance.

Yet now, all the threads weave together, forming a rainbow of colors. At the end waits the gold—the bees' honey. Such nourishment can't be ignored; good enough for the gods and goddesses, it is also good enough for me. And while I eat it, I'll be inspired to look more closely at what I've neglected, grateful for the bees that drew me into the attic, calling my attention to the treasures still waiting to be discovered.

HARCOURT

SIXTEEN

BEFORE I MARRIED M IN 1992 BUT WAS DATING HIM, I'D lived for ten years in San Rafael, California, in a charming one-bedroom cottage. Though it no longer exists, it does live on in my dreams, appearing frequently and in various configurations, making me wonder what symbolism it holds for me. But first, here is the story of what happened to that place.

The Harcourt Street House Isn't Just a Dream

At 9:00 am, during a Thanksgiving visit to my family in Calgary, I received a long-distance phone call from my then companion—now husband—M from California. We had been seeing each other for two years, and he usually called at night before we went to bed, so it was odd to hear from him in the morning.

He said, "I'm at your neighbor's place. There's been an accident."

His voice sounded strained, tight.

I asked, "What happened?"

"There's been a fire at your cottage."

"How bad?"

"Very bad. Everything's gone."

The fire suddenly was there, on that long-distance line, roaring out of control, eating up everything in its way, rushing on ahead. Like a wild animal that's been contained for too long, it was on the loose.

"Did Spook get out?" Spook was my beloved black cat.

"No. But the firemen say he would have died of smoke inhalation and not suffered. We've already buried him."

For ten years I'd rented that eighty-year-old cottage, the longest I'd lived anywhere. It sat under a canopy of trees in a quiet neighborhood of older houses, and from every window I saw green foliage. I could forget I lived a fifteen-minute walk from downtown San Rafael. I could forget I was in an urban area at all.

The cottage once was a guesthouse for one of the larger homes in a neighborhood flooded by elm trees. In the winter, I spent many nights in front of the fireplace, framed by built-in bookshelves, watching blue and yellow flames chase each other, never thinking then that similar flames would one day destroy my home. My eyes flickered over the well-used books overflowing the shelves, the subjects close to my heart: meditation, mythology, religion, psychology, dreams, poetry, art, fiction.

I'd found many of these texts in used bookstores, a habit I'd learned as a child from my grandpa. He'd taken me to Jaffe's Used Books in Calgary when I was barely tall enough to see over the tables that held comic books and old manuscripts. I remember the moldy smell of the place, mixed with oil they used on the wood floors. Books forever became associated for me with mildew, something decaying. But since I'd lived on a farm, decay wasn't a negative thing. I knew that rot could lead to new growth. Decay is part of a process, not the end of one, just as aging is.

Not long before he died, Grandpa came to me for help. He was renting a room in East Calgary. He didn't have contact with his sons or my mother, who wasn't living nearby at the time. Unable to speak because of a growth in his throat, he wrote me notes in perfect Pitman shorthand (he'd been a schoolmaster in Scotland until he moved to Canada in his early forties), asking for help. I called other family members, and we had him hospitalized.

But before he left, he gave me a book he was carrying in his hip pocket, *The Vicar of Wakefield.* He'd written notes to himself in it, my last link to him, something I treasured.

It had been on one of my bookshelves.

Over the years, I spent many uplifting hours in that cottage— reading, reflecting, writing. Taking time to prepare and eat tasty meals, to visit with friends, to have deep conversations. To paint, sculpt, play the piano and guitar—to sing. It was my sanctuary, and it had become M's as well.

When I first moved there, I had a dream welcoming me to the neighborhood. Neighbors brought me gifts, people I'd never seen before, and the feeling in the dream was very positive, as if I were part of a community. Even the trees welcomed me, leaves along the tree-lined street whispering, especially after dark.

For the first month, I sat up every night until after midnight, making floral curtains for the windows and French doors, decorating the house to fit its European country ambiance. Before moving in, I'd painted the kitchen and bathroom and cleaned every corner, claiming it as my own. T, my new neighbor and the person I paid rent to (his grandmother had lived there before I moved in) had put new linoleum on the kitchen floor.

A huge bay window gave me a view of the junipers, hawthorne, creeping baby roses, and hydrangeas growing in the front yard. And from there I could watch my neighbors working outside, learning their habits, their rhythms. They became part of mine.

I finished my first master's in the humanities while living there, leading to my teaching career. I also made a deeper commitment to writing by almost completing a second master's in creative writing before the fire happened, which I finished the following spring. But most important, M and I started our relationship while I was living in that house.

Over the years, I filled the cottage with my own artwork and that of my family. From one wall hung my youngest brother's relief of a horse pressing to be free of its frame. On another my own answering images hung, in dialogue with the gifts my sister had sent from Greece, Egypt, and other travels—an ancient cross with a place for candles, a hand-crafted kitchen witch that oversaw my cooking, a holder for fireplace matches. My mother's colorful, striped, hand-knitted tea cozies kept my teapot warm, and the things she made at the senior citizen's center—decoupage and heads of Beethoven and two children—made her a palpable presence.

I reconstructed my past in that place, reshaping an earlier time in my life in the things I kept around me. We all do this to a certain extent; I'm not suggesting that my impulse to do so was extraordinary. But I think a child from a broken home may need more reminders of family and friends. Consequently, I kept mementos over the years that could help me rebuild a life. I was the family historian, aware of the importance of letters, photos, and other keepsakes.

On my own after leaving Calgary at fifteen, from then on, I'd lived some distance from my Canadian home. With family members so far away, I treasured the things I'd collected that reminded me of them. One time I returned to California from a trip to Calgary with a lamp that had been in my room as a child. Not much else had survived from that time or place, so the lamp was even more precious. It had a black marble base, a bronze stem, and still appeared solid, though that home had long ago disintegrated.

Another time, my favorite uncle had insisted I take an old oil painting I admired that he'd brought with him from the Isle of Skye, his and my mother's birthplace. It was a still life, painted by an amateur but filled with character. The somber browns and blacks and umbers captured something of my uncle, a dour but lovable Scot who often seemed dark and brooding, longing for his homeland. In a way, he'd never left Scotland and represented that place for me.

Actually, when I say "home" and "family," I see how the impulse to construct one goes deep, deeper than I'd realized or understood until then. I not only had packed that house with memories—scrapbooks of my son's achievements and artwork, letters to and from family and close friends that went back to when I first left home, daily journals that I'd written in for years—but I'd tried in some way to reconstruct a family.

Unconsciously, I also had been recreating the gracious living that once filled the house I walked into at four years of age, the year Mother married Chester, my stepfather, and we moved to his farm. My inherited grandmother, my stepfather's mother, had taste and a developed sensibility. I'd never met her; I only had photographs, letters, her collections of china doll dishes and fine keepsakes, and my stepfather's stories to feed my imagination, to help me build a past that lived on in my cottage. But her spirit had somehow entered her belongings, and she became real to me—alive.

The Canadian writer Alice Munro claims that a woman is her home. If it's destroyed, more has been lost than just a few objects money can replace; a life has been grievously disrupted. Once I learned of the fire, my most immediate concerns, after my cat, were for my journals, writing projects, artwork, books, and photographs. If anything had held my "self," these things did. I felt I could survive the loss of personal belongings and eventually replace them. But the journals chronicled my daily life, a record of dreams and reflections, an ongoing dialogue with myself that provided an anchor in the midst of life's storms.

The writing projects—poetry, fiction, non-fiction—chronicled my artistic life and gave expression to my imagination. The artwork—sculpture, collages, paintings—captured a part of myself my writing couldn't. And the books I'd collected since I first developed an intellectual curiosity in my late teens each had my mark in them, passages underlined or highlighted, jottings in the margins, a record of my involvement with the authors and their ideas. It was intolerable to think I'd lost them too.

The photographs—I needn't explain their importance. It's the one thing everyone dreads losing. In my case, no one else had the pictures I'd rescued after the family had scattered so those images wouldn't be lost.

Fortunately, I had taken with me to Calgary the whole manuscript of a novel I was working on, aptly named *Traveling Light*. I'd hoped to find some time to write while I was there. *Traveling Light* gave me something, at least, to build on, a house of words that I could find shelter in. But it couldn't make up for the other losses.

Somehow, I got through that day after M's alarming call, moving around in a trance. I visited a walk-in clinic to get antibiotics for the bronchitis I was struggling with. I packed to go home, treasuring the few clothes I'd brought, now all the wardrobe I had. I tried to fathom my loss, but I couldn't comprehend what had happened. It didn't seem real. My adult son, mother, sister, brother-in-law, and brother all tried to comfort me, but I was inconsolable.

My son—whom I had driven to countless Little League and Babe Ruth games—said, "Geez, Mum, you've been thrown a curve." A curve? The image slammed into my mind, temporarily distracting me. All those years I'd watched him train to improve his pitching so he could throw wicked curves that would fool batters. It hadn't bothered me that the curves he threw might confuse other players, strike them out. But what did it mean that life had thrown me a curve? I didn't know I was up to bat.

I was unable to sleep all that night, prowling my sister's living room, flopping down on the sofa periodically and closing my eyes for a few minutes, trying to pass out. Thinking. All night thinking. Running over in my mind what had happened. Trying to imagine what the next day would bring when I would have to directly face my losses. I kept thinking of things that were gone, that I'd never see again, frantically trying to resuscitate them in my memory. If I could just hold them in my mind, they couldn't be destroyed.

Still, it was like losing a thousand loves at once—all the correspondence I'd saved over the years from family and friends, as valuable to me as my journals; the huge impressionistic painting I loved of a shoreline that hung in my bedroom; the print of *The Yellow Cow* by Franz Marc that M and I had bought at the Guggenheim on a recent trip to New York, a remembrance of that visit. I hadn't had a chance to frame it yet. The pictures of family I'd hung on my walls. So many sentimental things. Useless to anyone else. My life.

M met me at the San Francisco airport with a bouquet of flowers and his welcoming arms. We drove straight to San Rafael. Nothing could have prepared me for the burned out, blackened shell barely standing, for the utter ruin, a gaping hole in the street.

The city had blocked off the house and yard with orange plastic, like some crazy gift-wrapping, a touch of black humor. I stood there, looking into my former living room, feeling terribly exposed. The remains of my spinet piano leaned precariously on one leg. I slowly walked around the circumference of the house, trying to take it all in, contents of shelves and bureaus and closets dumped into the yard, much of it still sopping wet. I kept running into pages from journals or file folders, edges blackened, ink running. My words dissolving, pouring off the page.

Henry James claims our possessions are extensions of ourselves. In *The Portrait of a Lady,* he asks, "What shall we call our 'self'? Where does it begin? Where does it end? It overflows into everything that belongs to us—and then it flows back again."

But what happens if those things are destroyed? What happens then to one's self? Is it irrevocably damaged? How can it flow back again if the possessions that contained it are gone?

I suppose the fire could be seen as a preliminary run for my own death, this letting go of material possessions, the detachment. Isn't it the emptiness associated with death that fills us with dread? A coffin is empty until we fill it.

Several months later, I remembered something I'd totally forgotten about—my mother's wedding ring. She'd given it to me one Christmas when I also had been back in Calgary for a family visit. She'd said, "I want you to have this, Lily, in memory of me and your stepfather."

When I'd first put on the ring, I'd felt an overwhelming rush of emotion, as if I was somehow included in the circle of the ring. Recalling that it too had been destroyed, lost forever, I experienced another wave of grief. Mother had reset the stones, replacing two of the tiny diamonds with rubies my son's first long-term girlfriend had given her. The rubies reminded me of the garnets Mother had inherited from my stepfather's mother, set in a bracelet and earrings, one of the few things that had been rescued from an earlier fire on the farm where I had lived as a girl.

I'd looked at them longingly then, in love with their deep, red color and the dull luster of the stones. A fire seemed to burn inside them. I would put the bracelet around my tiny wrist and imagine being dressed elegantly, like the Victorian ladies I saw in old magazines that my stepfather's mother had kept.

After the Harcourt fire, I had denied losing the ring, blocking it from my memory. It represented all I had collected at Harcourt Street, the home I had finally created for myself out of fragments from my earlier life.

SEVENTEEN

GIVEN HOW MUCH THE HARCOURT STREET HOUSE HAD meant to me, it's no surprise that it has appeared in dreams many times during my work with Dr. Y. In its first appearance, M and I were living there. Its layout was pretty much the same as in actual life, but the rooms were larger. A female friend visited me at 10:30 at night with a young boy who might have been her grandchild. I was amazed that she was getting around so well after major hip surgery, but I didn't know what to serve them. It was too late for us to have a glass of wine together. Tea? I'm not sure what I settled on, but I was eager for her to see the new décor and believed she would appreciate the full effect of the lighting I'd put together that I was trying to turn on. But I was disturbed because M had moved some furnishings, and the changes were interfering with my aesthetics.

At the beginning of any relationship, especially a marriage, we tend to move one another's furnishings, inner or outer, shaking up the status quo. Sometimes we can't tolerate these adjustments and connections frazzle. In this case, I'm not willing to adjust to M's aesthetics, though the house has enlarged, making room for more than one person. Since Harcourt had been my place originally, and was essentially a one-person residence, I'm assuming it will continue to be under my control. Yet the dream is showing me something different.

This female friend who is visiting might be a clue. She's someone whose design sense I've always admired. Her homes are pristine, at the level of *Architectural Digest*. And even though she's had hip surgery, she's still able to navigate and visit me. The dream suggests that this aspect of myself that has strong aesthetic tendencies won't be shut out of this house, but I need to figure out what refreshments are appropriate for that hour of the night. I also must modulate how much input she has into the décor. If I let this super aesthetic part of myself take over, it doesn't leave room for either my preferences or M's.

Also, a lot of garbage has been building up inside for some reason. Usually, most people keep on top of their garbage by disposing of it frequently, not letting it build up. But here I'm not doing that, so does the garbage represent psychological material that I've ignored? Does it have anything to do with my relationship with M? Are there dynamics between us that we're not sorting through and need to be discarded?

In the dream, I was still getting used to the enlarged space and went into the bathroom to see what had changed there. I found a floor to ceiling window that could have left me exposed to the outer world, but someone had come up with an amazing invention—a curtain that could cover the whole thing or only parts. Thus, the guy I saw working outside the window couldn't see me when I activated the curtain/blind.

Here I'm on the verge of having my inner self penetrated. It makes me think how vulnerable writers are. They constantly reveal parts of themselves whether they write poetry, fiction, or non-fiction. These genres can't help but expose the author to the world. Yet this dream suggests there may be a way to not give everything to the viewer-reader. We are able to protect ourselves from being seen completely. While we can't avoid exposing ourselves somewhat in our writing, we also can take cover, perhaps behind the various personas we wear. So, while it might seem as if we're fully exposing ourselves, we do have ways to conceal what we're not ready to show.

Even though this house was my "heart court," a place that I associated with my single self and with females in general, I now share it with M, and he needs to do a better job of cleaning up his own messes. He had loved the cottage as much as I had, seeing it as a refuge as he went through his divorce and gave up his own home in the process. And he's the one who had to call and tell me it had burned to the ground. However, even though in the dream he's now living there with me, at times he isn't being sensitive to what my needs are in that space, and Harcourt continues to undergo transformations. Of course, this dream could be commenting on my inner masculine self that I identify with M. The M in the dream isn't necessarily the man I'm married to in actual life.

EIGHTEEN

MY HARCOURT STREET COTTAGE HAS MADE ANOTHER dream appearance. In this one, I'm living amidst major reconstruction at Harcourt Street. The interior and exterior have gone through massive changes that aren't completed yet, but I'm trying to make some order anyhow. I'm particularly fascinated by the lighting arrangement in the ceiling. It's a very inventive use of light to resemble the heavens and includes interesting patterns that look like constellations. An unfamiliar woman seems in charge of this work and these changes. At one point she says something about leaving a dead body in the house, but I protest, asserting that the smell will be too difficult to live with. I guess the body already is present, but it must be outside, and moving it will just make it more visible.

This view of Harcourt suggests that whatever it represents in my psyche is undergoing a transformation. Nothing is static. Reconstructing oneself seems to be ongoing. Of course, within the parameters of these changes, I try to manage the chaos they create.

Dr. Y wondered if this dream was showing the underside of the positive view I have of Harcourt. It's bringing the heavens— represented by the lighting arrangement in the ceiling—down into the ego's reality, but then there's this dead body. *Memento mori?* Life and death coexist. Yet I want to sanitize the smell. I want to push death aside, and this is true of me in conscious life as well. But, of course, it's part of life. There's no life without death, as much as I'd like to believe the opposite.

Dr. Y's comments remind me of the two Catrinas we have on our fireplace mantle in the actual home M and I share; Catrinas are the referential image of death in Mexico. Throughout Mexico, and even in American Hispanic communities, it's common to see Catrinas included in Day of the Dead celebrations.

They seem apt reminders of M's cancer diagnosis that we're living with. His living room chair, where he spends hours reading, is directly across from the mantel. I noticed recently that he'd shifted the dolls so their faces are turned away from him. Though he's now living closer to death, he's trying to face it little by little. It must be an immense transition for him to think that "I, too, am mortal" and not just in a theoretical way. It's immediate, creating a change in his consciousness.

This dream could be showing me, as with M's reaction to our Catrinas, that I'm also wanting to turn away from the reality that death could be visiting this Harcourt house, this place of the heart, if not actually, then as a possibility. The stench of death isn't far away, even though my beloved husband is still alive. I have to live with this potential reality as well as its stench. Death really does stink, not just literally in terms of a decaying body, but also figuratively. It stinks that we have to die!

NINETEEN

Afew years after the Harcourt Street fire, at the home M and I share in a city miles away from where the fire happened, I cut through potato vines climbing our backyard shed. In it, I'd stored some items that miraculously survived the destruction. The vines reminded me of fairy tales where brambles conceal some treasure. But these plants have no brambles. They're just prolific, growing as quickly as I cut them back—like dreams that seem to come from a never diminishing source.

Once inside the shed, I dug out my old Tarot deck. The box containing the cards was blackened, obliterating any markings, but the cards themselves were intact, edges tinged with brown. Excitement bubbled up in my stomach. Fingering this familiar deck that I hadn't seen since the fire made me feel connected again to my former cottage, a place I loved more than any place I've lived. Surrounded by trees, it had a fairy-tale quality to it. A fifty-foot-tall pine grew in the backyard, and a Hawthorne tree in front blossomed each spring, competing with the baby rose vine that climbed the white fence and hung over the porch.

I slipped the Tarot deck into my pocket. Back in our study, I sat on the love seat and shuffled the major arcana. A pungent odor rose from the cards, a mixture of mildew and smoke, reminding me of that nightmare time when for several days I dug in blackened ruins, trying to rescue five years of journals that I'd stored in the closet that, unfortunately, came to be right next to the heart of the fire. I couldn't bear losing those records completely, but it was a hopeless task. They were severely burned, the edges just black ash, interiors soaked with water from fire hoses, in some instances the ink washed away. Yet I didn't give up until I'd recovered every page I could find.

Now dried out, they wait in the shed, containing the remnants of that time in my life, as well as what's left of scrapbooks I kept of my son's accomplishments; remains of letters I'd received over the years from family and friends; files of papers I'd written during my own college years, so hard won as a single parent. I couldn't face letting go of those chronicles completely, hoping that one day I'd find a way to make copies of them so they could be restored to their rightful place inside my current home. Fortunately, I'd kept the rest of my diaries— dating from the early seventies when I began this inner journey—in a sturdy trunk located some distance from the heart of the fire. They only suffered smoke damage.

My fingers, having a mind of their own at times, selected a Tarot card at random for me to meditate on for the next few months. The Moon turned up. I stared at the images on the card: a lobster—or maybe it's a crab, often associated with the moon—swims in the water. Above it, two yellow dogs crouch under the smiling face in the moon, red tongues hanging out, water drops appearing to originate in the golden moon above them. Are the dogs the moon's earthly representative, their ancestors the wolves howling at a full moon? Or is that apocryphal? Are they related to my moon maiden who appeared in a dream not long after I started working with Dr. Y? The corners of two castles frame the animals, visible in the background. The dogs seem to be lapping up the big water drops with their tongues, as if they have a great thirst.

I can understand their thirst for the moon and its mysteries, so magical, constantly changing, and yet so reliable in its repeating cycles, seeming to be connected to the animal nature many of us have lost contact with. Still, I want to push the card away. Can't I come up with something more original? The devil or the wheel of fortune?

But I must accept the moon—various and fluid. What changes does this image foreshadow in me? How am I like the moon, waxing and waning?

Given my association of Harcourt with female consciousness, the house and what it represents seems to fit into this moon imagery, an astronomical body orbiting the earth. Like the moon, my dream Harcourt is going through many phases. No wonder that over the years it has appeared in many dreams and continues to go through major renovations.

In this particular dream, the ceiling seems to have been raised, and bookshelves loaded with books line one wall, the top shelves so high I'll need a tool to reach them. But I love having my library expanded in this way, and the colorful book covers give life to the room. I'm figuring out how to arrange the interior space with my current furniture, but it still needs considerable work before I can actually move in.

A former female colleague shows up in the dream. She's lost all of her excess weight, and we greet each other enthusiastically with hugs. Then she changes into a man who has a young boy and is interested in a relationship with me.

The overweight woman who appears in the dream, a mother figure, has actually lived in the Harcourt neighborhood, so it makes sense that she's there now—though transformed. A leaner version of herself, she seems closer to how she probably was originally, a return to her more natural self. And then she becomes a man who expresses interest in me, suggesting the fluid nature of our masculine and feminine identities, a phenomenon that young people today are much more aware of and, hence, the arrival of a new pronoun to describe these individuals: they.

Like this woman, the house also had been transformed. It's no longer recognizable, suggesting it can't return to what it was, and neither can I. I'm also changed and have different perceptions and motivations.

Dr. Y wondered if things in my inner world that are close to my heart court (Harcourt) are in flux. The dream implies that something in me is undergoing a transition and isn't ready to be inhabited fully, but it has great potential. The old identity could be experiencing a major shift. The house and this former colleague are shapeshifting.

My response? I feel trapped by all these changes going on outside of my control. We have so little power over our destiny, and so many things can happen that we wouldn't choose. No wonder I feel trapped. This dream also might be reflecting my emotional state in response to what M and I are facing externally. Cancer has entered our lives and there's no predicting where it will take us. Everything is shapeshifting, and it's exhausting to work my way through the changes.

During this session with Dr. Y, I was recovering from a bad cold and feeling tired because I wasn't sleeping well (this was pre-COVID-19). Our family doctor had recommended rest, but I hate lying around and resisted her recommendation. Of course, it also makes me think of the worst. Scary thoughts intrude, making me wonder if something worse has invaded my body, and I'll end up like M with cancer. For me, it's like lifting the lid on Pandora's box, releasing all of my most negative fears.

I also was becoming more aware of my own aging process, the groaning joints that whisper to me "your body is declining." I have little actual control over how anything will play out. All I can do is continue my full exercise routine as long as possible and hope to quiet the groaning body parts.

TWENTY

HARCOURT SEEMS TO CAPTURE THE CENTER OF MY FEMININE identity, and the following dream reinforces this idea: I've been away from Harcourt for some time. While I was gone, a fellow fiction writer, L, has stayed there and now is moving out. I've returned after this absence and spend much of the night there, discovering that quite a few changes have happened to the cottage in my absence. It's much larger, with higher ceilings and bigger rooms than before. In the bedroom, one wall is slanted and terraced with a variety of items that I don't completely recall. I plan to leave them there as decorations.

Curious to look out the windows at the top of the wall that runs its width, I climb a kind of ladder and am surprised to see that the ocean reaches to just below the window, but it only appears to be on that side of the house.

I'm extremely busy removing things and rearranging the place to my satisfaction. There's a lot to do, but I'm also delighted with the changes I'm discovering as well as having the house back. L tried to help as best she could before she left.

I also discover that the mailbox is full, there being letters addressed to Lily Soucie, my former husband's surname, as well as Lily MacKenzie, a family name I claimed after I married my current husband.

There are lots of lights in this place that I want to adjust and turn on regardless of what the electrical bill will be. I love the illumination.

This dream left an aftereffect all day long, leaving me feeling spacy, as if I were submerged in the ocean I found outside this transformed cottage. If the ocean is symbolic of the unconscious, I was really immersed in it today, and I'm now living right next to it in this revamped Harcourt house. I'm left with so much to sort through: all of these objects appearing on a slanted wall; the many lights that I want to turn on; and so much else to explore, some of which I will keep. And then there is L, this other female writer who has been a placeholder while I was away from Harcourt and who shares the same first letter to her name as I do: "L."

L writes mainly fiction and non-fiction, so she lives more in prose than in poetry. Has this writer self, who focuses on short and long fiction, established herself now in those modes while living in this space and is able to move on, Harcourt having enlarged to contain the energy she represents?

I'm curious about all this mail waiting for me and addressed to both Soucie and MacKenzie. I actually used the name Soucie from my previous marriage when I lived at this address. After I married M, I didn't want to take on another man's name, so I chose MacKenzie, a family name from my mother's Scottish heritage. So, the mail seems to represent different phases of my life and different versions of myself, and I can receive that mail now in this special place. I'm receiving communications to various versions of Lily.

Dr. Y noted that Harcourt seemed to be a place where I could collect all parts of myself and finally come into my own. And it really is a heart court.

It seems important that M doesn't live there with me. It appears to be my own private space, and there's much more to learn about it when I turn on all of the lights and can better see what awaits me. This Harcourt dream is talking about expansion that will enlarge on my current identity.

TWENTY-ONE

THANKSGIVING, TWENTY-TWO YEARS AFTER THE HARCOURT fire, I dreamt about my former home. It's amazing how the psyche remembers these things so accurately.

I spent much of the night moving back into an enlarged Harcourt house, with an upstairs that was pretty complete. I didn't go up there to look around until I started talking to Sharon, a former girlfriend of the man I was then dating in the dream world (I don't know this Sharon in my waking life). His identity wasn't clear to me, and he wasn't someone I knew in actual life, but I didn't mind being friends with his former girlfriend. He seemed to be a reader and not a particularly social person, hanging back while the women interacted. She needed a place to store some things, and I thought of offering space in the upstairs that I hadn't visited yet. In my kitchen, I loved the antique stove I saw there, one that had been converted from woodstove to gas.

Upstairs, I was blown away by how complete that unit was, as spacious as the downstairs with windows all around that gave a 360-degree view of the area, including a pond or some other water feature. There also was a balcony that I stepped out on, but my weight caused the house to tip a bit, and I quickly went back inside, warning others not to use it. It appeared as if whoever had done the construction or owned the house had planned to have someone live on this second level because they'd left another antique stove there as well as kitchen items, though there weren't proper room partitions set up to accommodate such things.

I decided that since the only bathroom was downstairs, where I was living, I didn't want someone moving into the second level and sharing my facilities. So, for the time being, it would remain a storage unit that I controlled.

I've been reading more of Henry Corbin's metaphysical works that focus on mystical hermeneutics. His writings describe higher spiritual levels, giving me access to the kind of uninterrupted 360-degree view described in this dream. It offers a more inclusive outlook, just as his thinking is expansive and incorporates several religious traditions. From this perspective, I'm more able to see the underlying unity of things. But there also seems to be a problem if I step onto the balcony rather than remaining contained inside this higher dimension. Otherwise, I can shake up the whole house. Perhaps esoteric ideas do shake us up, offering unusual ways of understanding our time on this planet.

My man friend/partner in the dream, some aspect of my masculine identity—or *animus* in Jung's parlance—is more introverted, a reader, and happy to be left out of the women's conversation. Through him, I make a new female friend, a woman he'd previously been involved with. So not only am I experiencing a revamped Harcourt, but I'm also getting to know a new feminine aspect of myself that this male has introduced me to.

I actually identify with this man's perspective. I'm fine with having people around, but I don't necessarily want them to live with me. Nor am I always eager for chatting if my mind is on something else. I can mingle with all these different perspectives, but I want to have my own base and control it to a certain degree. I want to know who comes in and who goes out. I also value my privacy and don't want to share my bathroom. Though this cottage now has an upper level and has been somewhat enlarged, it's still a limited space and most appropriate for one person.

Dr. Y pointed out that though fire destroys, it also transforms. While the actual Harcourt house that I lived in no longer exists, in my psyche it has become the *imago* of the place. The intrapsychic house that went through the fire's calcination is still alive. It revisits me just as I revisit it in memory and in dreams. The place, and what it represents, is still forming, just as I am. And there is always something new to discover both in this former residence as well as in our identities. If the cells in our bodies renew every seven years, then why wouldn't the person inhabiting such a body go through similar transformations? The body is plastic, and so is the psyche.

TWENTY-TWO

IN THE FINAL HARCOURT DREAM THAT I'LL WRITE ABOUT IN this volume—though not the last one I'll have of this place—I seemed to have outgrown Harcourt for now. I was living with M in an older place like Harcourt. We'd decided to have some work done on part of the house, even though we didn't own it. It hadn't been put together well originally, so taking measurements and doing all of the "right" things now was difficult for the construction boss. They were well into the work when it occurred to me that we should have told the owner first and gotten permission to make changes. But someone in the dream said, "We're doing the owner a favor, and the changes we're making aren't enduring."

I was amazed at how quickly the work got done. Pretty much overnight. And the outcome was very attractive. The contractor had chosen black trim on white background. At some point, I was interacting with Del Potro, the Argentinian tennis player. I made the conscious decision in the dream to have an affair with him while married to M and believed I could pull off the deception. It was an unusual stance for me to take, but I believed that at my age I was allowed to do something out of the ordinary.

Del Potro and I had a conversation about couples needing to function as a single person does in the sense that individually each should have separate interests and even take separate trips at times. If there was enough trust (bad word given I was cheating on M with Del Potro in the dream) between them, then such an arrangement should work fine. Meanwhile, there was a lot of cleaning up to do after these renovations.

So here is the Harcourt house in a different aspect. I've come to view it as a feminine space, but Del Potro shows that a man can also have that "heart court" presence.

He plays tennis and shows a lot of heart when he meets with his colleagues. A big bear of a guy, in the clubhouse, he's one of the most adored players and, apparently, a very sweet man.

Meanwhile, I'm impressed with how the workers have incorporated the opposites, like the yin and yang symbol, by using black and white paint. Representing both feminine and masculine modes, black associated with feminine and white with masculine, both contain the other. The colors also remind me of newsprint or text in a book, with black usually conveying letters and white the page. Is this dream suggesting that there's a shift within my psyche so that the house I once connected to my female roots now embraces both male and female?

Cheating on M is not something I would do in conscious life, but it seemed a good solution in this dream. Dr. Y pointed out that some of the boundaries we keep in the outer world don't apply in dreams. If we were to do in our conscious lives what we do in dreams, people would really get hurt. He said, "That isn't true in the inner world where you can have relationships with two kinds of masculine *imagos* who are very different, but both compliment you. Your ideal man may be many men or many kinds of masculine energy that you have relationships with." So, this expanded Harcourt allows me to expand internally. I'm able to embrace everything I value about M and our lives together. At the same time, I can also connect with this Del Potro type.

I like the broadening and inclusiveness that this dream suggests is possible.

ART

TWENTY-THREE

WHEN I REALIZE THAT MANY PARTS OF MYSELF HAVEN'T YET reached consciousness or been fully realized, it's like saying goodbye to aborted children. The tragedy? There aren't enough years ahead of me to be able to accomplish what I haven't done so far, making me a kind of Medea because I haven't given full birth to my potential.

Medea visited me recently. Her two dead sons were not trailing behind, seeking revenge. And Jason was nowhere to be seen. Medea herself seemed redeemed, her face unlined, a calm serenity in her manner. She wore a stylish red dress trimmed with floral piping. Her shapely body reminded me of full-bodied Italian women. She seemed built not just to give life but also to enjoy it. Her black hair coiled around her neck, a mysterious river that beckoned.

If I were to take off on that river, what would I find at the end? A heart of stone? A pyramid of possibilities? A woman who had used her power in the only way she could?

When I saw Euripides's play *Medea* many years ago, I was already in her spell. Her myth resonated for me as it still does for many women. She is our Medea, our savior—a woman unafraid of accepting her power and acting on it as necessary. One of Lilith's symbolic daughters. According to legend,

> Adam tried to make Lilith lie beneath him during sexual intercourse. Lilith would not meet this demand of male dominance. She cursed Adam and hurried to her home by the Red Sea. Adam complained to God, who then sent three angels, Sanvi, Sansanvi, and Semangelaf, to bring Lilith back to Eden. Lilith rebuffed the angels by cursing them. While by

the Red Sea, Lilith became a lover to demons and produced one hundred babies a day. The angels said that God would take these demon children away from her unless she returned to Adam. When she did not return, she was punished accordingly. And God also gave Adam the docile Eve.[11]

I talked to my sister this morning, and we reminisced about our mother who died when she was 101, trying to focus on her positive attributes: the insatiable zest for life: the curiosity and willingness to travel well into her nineties, the compassion for those in need, the ability to somehow communicate her love while also abandoning us at times.

We mothers are all Medeas in some way, wounding and even killing parts of our children. Sometimes we destroy the whole child, forced into this behavior by our own limited lives that we then pass on, constrained either by the culture we grew up in, by our families, or by all of the above.

My grandmother was one of those women. She left Portree, Isle of Skye, after WWI ended to join her husband, a Scottish schoolmaster, in Canada. He had fled to the new world before the war to find a better life for all of them. Seven years later, unable until then to safely make the ocean crossing, she and their four children—three boys and a girl—joined him, arriving in Calgary during a snowstorm.

To go from the warmth of the family womb in Portree, with uncles, aunts, cousins, friends, a charming village, to this frigid climate on the barren prairies must have been a jolt. Was it revenge at being forced to leave her home that encouraged her to abandon her husband and kids after a year and find work for herself with a family in Calgary's Mount Royal district? She must have been furious with my grandfather for making her join him. He also was a difficult man, his tongue stinging as much as his slaps. She refused to tolerate his abuse any longer.

In the 1920s, it took guts and daring for a woman to desert her husband and kids. It took even greater nerve to travel to Mexico City with her lover—her employer. Some might claim she had a psychotic break, but this interpretation is too clinical. Menopause madness? More plausible. But why do we need to assert a woman is mad or unbalanced if she chooses to leave her kids and an inattentive, abusive husband? Some children drive their parents to drink. Some aren't lovable, and she had just spent seven years as a single parent, fully responsible for all her kids' needs. What if she got fed up with the whole mess and wanted a life for herself before it was too late? Or did she have a premonition she would die young—four years after she arrived in Mexico—and decided to do as much living as she could in the meantime?

And what of the Nigerian girls that have been abducted from their schools? What kind of life had they imagined for themselves after books opened doors to them that had previously not existed? Their minds and imaginations no longer could be confined to the rigors of rural life and the demands of women in those societies. They might talk back to the men in their lives and refuse to follow the traditional path. They might find in their hearts a desire to be independent—full human beings. "Why are fanatics so terrified of girls' education? Because there's no force more powerful to transform a society. The greatest threat to extremism isn't drones firing missiles, but girls reading books."[12]

The day I dropped out of school, there was no eclipse of the sun or moon. The color didn't drain from the expansive prairie sky. No one rushed up to me and shouted, "You're making a serious mistake you'll later regret." At the beginning of grade eleven, during mid-November snow flurries, I fled Calgary's Crescent Heights High School. No more three-mile treks each way in sub-zero temps. No more rising at dawn and shivering through the morning rituals of dressing, eating, and fighting with my two younger brothers before leaving the house.

It was 1955, and I had my first taste of freedom.

Okay, stepfathers are easy targets. Mine was no exception. But he earned my spleen. He had made it clear for some time that women didn't need an education. He pointed out that he only completed the eighth grade, claiming an education was wasted on a girl who would just get married and have kids. I believed him. Heaven forbid that kids might have mothers who could read, write, and converse beyond a few grunts at the dinner table.

I was too young and naive to realize that his lack of higher education locked him into a laborer's life, first as a farmer and then as a rock crusher at the local rock-crushing plant. Some days he came home so exhausted that he couldn't eat dinner. Instead, he crashed on the floor, later arousing himself long enough to crawl into bed and do it again the next day. That should have set off rockets in my mind, signaling his life lacked something.

It didn't.

Not then.

It seemed normal to live a proscribed life.

And my mother's response to me dropping out of school? She had dropped out herself, though not from school. A few weeks earlier, she had fled to the coast—Vancouver—to join her lover. Would she have wanted me to continue school? Theoretically, yes. She believed in girls being educated, though she didn't go beyond high school herself. So did her father, my grandfather, a schoolmaster before he left Scotland for Canada in the early 1900s. But neither was around then to cause me to reconsider.

After Mum left, I had the crazy idea that my two younger brothers needed me at home to cook and clean and iron. I had some noble Florence Nightingale image of myself caring for the needy, not realizing I also was deprived. I would devote myself to my brothers and stepfather, using them as an excuse for dropping out. Stepping into the caretaker role assuaged my guilt for letting myself down and pre-empting a future.

My sister, six years older than I, may have tried to dissuade me from jumping off the deep end. But there was a wide gulf between us at that point. We had shared a bedroom until she married when I was thirteen. I not only stole money out of her hope chest, but I also borrowed her clothes without asking and returned them to the closet soiled. This behavior didn't endear me to her. She wanted me out of her hair. She also was deeply involved in her own life by then, working as a secretary for an oil company while her husband articled as an accountant through a correspondence course.

For all my good intentions, I wasn't ready to become an instant mother, another example of letting myself and others down. I struggled each morning to drag myself out of bed. Actually, it was a struggle just to wake up. My immediate impulse was to silence the alarm, plant the pillow over my head, and go back to sleep.

Sometimes I did just that, not wanting the responsibility for waking my brothers, making their breakfast, packing a lunch for each, and sending them off to school. Quickly my justification for quitting school was dissolving. So was the notion I had of rescuing my stepfather and brothers. I failed yet again.

In "Through a Glass Darkly," Christopher Vasillopulos asks: "What moved Medea away from her role as a healer, as an expression of the Great Mother, to her role as a child-killer, a ghastly expression of the Terrible Mother? What moved Medea from a positive transformative figure to a negative one, from a giver of life to a dealer of death?" Vasillopulos answers these questions when he says, "Any woman capable of reason and passion would have rebelled, in one way or another, from any social order that limited her options to the point of denying her fundamental nature."[13]

Medea rebelled. Unable to participate in the heroic myth, to take the hero's journey herself and embrace all her potential, she became a Terrible Mother instead of a Great Mother. She had no choice but to destroy the sons she had given birth to rather than have Jason, their ne'er-do-well father, run off with them.

My son was born when I had just turned seventeen. I stayed with his dad for six months after the birth, yet I knew if I stayed in that marriage, my future would be bleak. From the beginning, my then husband spent Friday nights after his workweek was over in the bar with his buddies, partying. I was supposed to accept this behavior. Suck it up. Be a docile wife. Not complain.

I complained.

I didn't like playing second fiddle to his friends. I also couldn't face having more kids with this man and not receiving his affection. Somehow, I sensed there might be more in life for me than the traditional working-class marriage. That knowledge eventually prevailed.

After returning to work as a receptionist and hiring someone to care for my baby, I knew I could support us without a husband. And I did. I would like to say we lived happily ever after and I became the responsible adult I was destined to be. Neither would be true.

Constantly moving, either I messed up, the people I shared apartments or houses with became impossible, or both. While I always managed to find office work and later cocktail waitressing, which paid more, often taking on two jobs to support us, I was barely making it on all levels. I didn't receive child support from my ex, except for an occasional $15 a month when I pressed for it. Something in me wanted more than a prosaic life, but I still didn't know how to achieve it without a high school diploma or any obvious way to earn one. I only had time for working, caring for my son, and partying when I had a chance. Anything else seemed closed to me.

I can't undo the pain I caused my son because of my youth and my occasional unwise behavior at that time. Cosmetic surgery can't remove the scars or the bad memories. However, I can now see this period in perspective, part of a learning process that propelled me into the 1960s and a new way of thinking and feeling. I didn't need to live out my life as an underachiever, a failure. With the help of others—my sister, friends, college teachers, and therapists—I moved forward, not bound by the past or my own apparent limitations.

I had a dream recently during which I realized I had latent qualities I hadn't developed and was feeling awful about it. I recall thinking in the dream that if I were younger and not heading toward my eighties, I would have time to fill in the gaps. But it seemed cruel and depressing to become aware of my failings then. Here are the aborted children, the dormant abilities or talents I didn't have time to explore. It's jolting to think that my psyche has kept track and wants to be heard, even at this late date.

Or maybe the date isn't so late.

Many assume that once we reach a certain age, growth stops, and our later years don't count for all that much. It's just a matter of marking time, waiting for death to claim us. But this dream doesn't seem to share that perspective. By calling attention to the problem, it suggests there is still time to evolve. I needn't think in terms of shutting down. There are always roads not taken in our lives—possibilities, side streets, detours. Circumstances and our own limitations often prevent us from pursuing these multiple paths. But it doesn't mean we can't pick up some earlier threads we weren't able to pursue previously and follow them. We may not fully accomplish what we might have at a younger age; after all, I'm not going to get that fine arts degree and become a professional visual artist. Yet I can embellish on the skills I have and express satisfactorily a talent I haven't had time to pursue until now.

And that's the gift Medea can give us: out of immediate necessity, the Medea in us may kill certain possibilities before we have a chance to know they exist. But I believe she also can exercise her powers in more fruitful ways. She can give and support life as well as take it away, evoking the opposite of the Terrible Mother. When we fulfill ourselves, we give Medea the opportunity to be redeemed and help restore the power that naturally belongs to her.

TWENTY-FOUR

A S MENTIONED EARLIER, THE VISUAL ARTS CONTINUE TO
attract me. In my forties, I took numerous art classes at the
College of Marin whenever I had extra time: drawing, painting, and
sculpting. This interest, that developed later in my life, has taken
a secondary role to writing, but it remains alive. I'm sure that if I
hadn't had a child and my more bohemian self had appeared earlier,
I would have been a visual artist as well as a writer. In painting, I've
explored watercolors as well as acrylics and oils. When I sit at my
art table and play with color, I don't have any preconceived idea of
what I'll work on. The unconscious leads me, and I pick out shades
as I go along without notions of the outcome.

At times, I start by permeating the watercolor paper with water.
Then I drop color into the liquid and watch it choose a path—or
many paths. Eventually, I'll add other colors and let them mingle,
creating hues I wouldn't have discovered if I hadn't been open to
surprise. These explorations fill me with joy because I don't have
expectations of where I'll end up. A similar thing happens when I'm
writing because I never know where each day's forays will take me.
It's one of the reasons I so enjoy doing it.

During these art interludes, I'm able to escape my writer self
and fully play with color and form and materials. I particularly like
letting the unconscious speak to me in this way, at times trusting this
medium more than language for engaging with my inner world. I
have less control over the content and am continually surprised by
what surfaces. It's a little like viewing a living Rorschach.

Representational work doesn't interest me; my creations tend to be
abstract. But if I look at what has appeared via my hand onto canvas
or watercolor paper, subtle shapes begin to emerge, as happens when

I watch clouds in the sky. They don't set out to suggest particular images, but often they do. Nonfigurative art intrigues me the most because it isn't necessarily determined by what I'm visually seeing in the outer world, though I'm sure there is a connection—external objects influence me somewhat especially in terms of color and forms. Therefore, what I create in this medium seems to portray another dimension of myself, one I otherwise wouldn't be aware of.

I believe that's one way the unconscious speaks to all of us. When I look around our house at the many paintings I've done that are propped on bookshelves or hung on walls, the dominating element is the dynamic force within the frame. If you can call brush strokes energetic (and a brush isn't always the implement that I use to create effects), mine are, as are the colors I pursue. I tend to include everything on the color wheel. And a brush isn't the only implement that I use to make what's contained within the frame feel alive and in motion.

Given my ease with not having a preplanned destination, I wonder why dying frightens me so much. Since I like surprises in making art, why doesn't that attitude carry over for the end game we all face, except death marks the end of our days on this earth, and, apparently, there is no return from it. When I'm playing with art materials, I don't have those worries and can embrace the unknown. Even so, I wish I could apply this attitude toward what the future may hold. Then maybe death won't seem so dreadful. But it's something I'll have to consciously work on.

Because of this early interest in the visual arts, I had planned in my seventies to enroll in art classes so I could focus more on developing that part of my brain. Having taught rhetoric for over thirty years at the University of San Francisco, I had more than enough tuition remission credits to use if I wanted to enroll in USF's art department. I liked the idea of building a new foundation as a visual artist, yet I had no desire to work toward another degree or be graded for my efforts.

When I discussed this option with Dr. Y, he wondered if I was seeking more of a beginners' mind, seeking to bring that attitude to whatever I decided to do in the visual arts and approach it as if for the first time. He thinks we bring freshness to our endeavors if we take such an attitude to everything we do.

Yet while I sought the discipline of taking structured art classes, ones that most students enroll in so they can get a BFA, I had no desire to put myself through such a program. The weightiness of officially becoming a visual artist or getting a degree left me cold. Still, I also wanted the status of completing such a discipline. So, I was in a quandary. While I wanted to challenge myself, I also was not willing to go the extra mile to do so. And while arts and crafts activities at senior centers are valuable for lots of people, they didn't offer the complexity I was seeking. As Dr. Y pointed out, "You don't want to be ordinary."

And it's true. I don't want to just be another old woman taking art classes to enrich her life, though there's nothing wrong with that activity. Why do I have to set myself apart? It's because I'm ambitious. I wouldn't have earned a GED in my early twenties so I could attend community college and eventually earn two graduate degrees if I weren't determined to succeed at what I do.

Whatever I attempt, I apply myself fully. Even in my sessions with Dr. Y, I'm striving to be a good analysand. He pointed out that this heroic quest that still occupies me usually is our task in the first half of life, while the second half is more of an inward quest. But I resist the idea that there's a template for the first and second half of life that we need to fit into. Since much of the first half of my life was spent just surviving, raising myself and my son without help from his biological father or others, it wasn't until my forties that I was able to finally accomplish some of the things I otherwise might have attempted when I was younger.

For me the question was: what's my goal with art? Was I after a new version of the same old thing? Or did the urge come from a deeper place in me that needed to be honored? Dr. Y wondered if an old thing I've done in the past, like artwork, could become new in terms of how I actually do it. That approach offered another perspective for me to consider.

But I also have trouble accepting the idea that we old people somehow need to be entertained, amused, or distracted as we're waiting for death to claim us. There seems to be an assumption that we're no longer able to direct our lives once we've fulfilled our role as parents and grandparents. Dr. Y believes it's possible we can grow into a kind of wisdom, and there are deeper transcendent aspects of life that are more than just this personality or life story. Ultimately, all of us are ordinary, but is there something in me that has a spark of transcendence? Do I have a meaning or purpose that can make me feel vital and fresh, a beginner?

I realized I'd had a dream that spoke to our discussion, and I described it: I was flying and tremendously enjoying the feeling it gave me to levitate at will and stay aloft without much effort. It had been a long while since I'd had a flying dream, something that happened frequently when I was younger. I loved the sensation of being aloft in dreams, using only my arms and legs to move through the air. Sometimes I could do it without much movement at all. This flying self seems to be an essential part of my being, and I think art makes me feel as if I'm airborne, a winged creature.

After I discussed the dream with Dr. Y, I wondered if the soaring I loved was a result of me planning to stop tutoring at USF and take an art class instead. The exhilaration it gave me felt as if something had freed me from being so grounded and married to the earth. Was there a connection with me being a Libra, an air sign? I'm skeptical about astrology, but I'm also willing to consider some of these popularized ideas.

Dr. Y didn't dismiss my association and speculated that for me to fly so easily and freely, to have such an effortless relationship with the air, could be appropriate to some aspect of who I am. That comment led me to share another dream I felt was connected to our conversation: I was caring for K's fourth child. In actual life, K is a gifted poet and was part of a poetry group I attended for many years. She has a strong *puella aeterna* quality. Therefore, even as an older woman, she's not grounded and lives on the edge financially and otherwise.

I asked Dr. Y if "fourth" means anything. He pointed out that Jung says four is a quaternary, a symbol of wholeness. I said K has squared a circle with the baby, a child she doesn't have any interest in spending time with. But I did. In the dream, the child was only about three months old yet already amazingly mature. If I held his hands, he could stand already by holding on to me. Later, I found him calling someone on the phone about problems he had viewing the TV. However, he had the phone turned the wrong way, so I helped him with that. Once connected to technical support, he articulated perfectly his problems with the TV in clear, grammatically correct sentences, amazing for someone his age.

I took the phone at one point and told the woman on the other end about the child and how old he was. I seemed prepared to take over as his mother and realized it was fortunate that I was going to stop tutoring as I would need that time to keep up with his growth.

I noticed his hands and feet were larger than usual, so it appeared he would be a big man. Does this baby represent some part of my masculine self whose actual mother is a poet/writer?

This child was a delight to be with, a constant source of discovery. I never knew what he would do next, which reminds me of what happens both when I play with paint and when I write: I never know what's coming, the activity being a constant source of discovery.

The dream child, K's fourth, seems precocious and wise, but at first, he doesn't know how to communicate very well. And he needs help conveying his needs. Even though he's advanced in many ways, he needs nurturance and guidance.

When Dr. Y and I gave more thought to who had given birth to this remarkable baby, I realized I needed to explore more what role K plays in my life. During a previous session, K had appeared in another dream, but in the later one, she seemed more mature and complete. She seems to represent a part of my own feminine writer identity who is fulfilling herself.

While this fourth child can't use the phone and communicate what he knows to the other in the dream, he does learn how to hold and use it as a means for sending and receiving messages. Yet the reason for him using the phone in the first place is because he is having problems viewing the TV set, and the TV is another form of communicating larger social things. The child realizes there's a problem with that mode, and he wants to connect with someone who can help him fix it. In the dream, the TV also could represent communication that's trying to come through from one part of the psyche to another and is not fully mastered, not fully set up. Channels are not open enough. It sounds correctable, but it needs attention. And that involves me becoming more conscious of the situation so I can act!

It appears as if I'm wanting this woman at the other end to know what an amazing child this is. With his hands and feet being larger than usual, it suggests he's going to be a real presence, not ordinary. And that speaks to what I was getting at earlier about art classes. Perhaps this baby represents the beginning of a new aspect that's trying to surface in me. Communication seems an important aspect of this child's development. Already he's trying to reach out over the phone to this woman. As a writer, that's also what I'm trying to do, to reach those beyond my usual range.

TWENTY-FIVE

TODAY I STUMBLED ON THE SCULPTURE THAT I CARVED OUT of stone when I was taking art classes at the College of Marin several years ago. An oval shape of about ten inches, it mainly shows what resembles an elephant's head, its trunk winding around it. At the time, I told some friends I was giving birth to an elephant. One of them said, "But that could take years!" She was right. Elephants have long gestation periods. But no one asked how it was possible for me to give life to one.

Freeing this elephant image became both a challenge and an exhilarating process for me, although at times releasing it was tedious, physically tiring, and often frustrating. Would I be able to give it shape? Capture its essence so that others could also see it?

On good days, the work proceeded as a meditation, allowing me to reflect on the relationship between my involvement with the stone and the aging process. During these periods, I frequently asked myself: "Has aging a meaning?" The question chipped away at me as I chiseled and filed the stone. Often all I was left with were small mounds of fine shavings and a few larger, more meaningful chunks. These were the answers I received.

With another birthday quickly approaching, and a corresponding increase in the physical signs of aging—more wrinkles, gray hair, and osteoarthritic joints—it's natural that I would be preoccupied with this question. Finding an answer, or answers, seems crucial in order to move forward confidently into what euphemistically has been called the "golden years." Are they really golden, and if so why?

Of course, when I ask the question—has aging a meaning?—I'm also asking the ultimate question: Does life have a meaning? Does my life have meaning?

In an article entitled "Aging: On the Way to One's End," Jungian analyst Ann Belford Ulanov observes that "Aging means more than fear and infirmity and death. It touches all the large questions of life. What is our end? To what goal are we moving? What purpose guides us? When we come to an end, at what end shall we have arrived? Aging presses these questions upon us throughout our lives."[14] By asking the question "has aging a meaning," I'm assuming it does, just as I assume life is more than the minutes we pass on this earth.

Could aging's purpose be to force us to confront the evidence of our aging? Of course, in the process I'm also forced to confront myself: Who am I? Why am I here?

Just as the Greeks consulted the Oracle at Delphi when they had big questions, I turned again to my elephant and the process of releasing it from the stone.

In the sculpture studio, I was fascinated not only with my own emerging creation, but with the intense concentration of the other sculptors on their work. As they bent over their pieces, shoulders hunched and bodies alert to every nuance, I realized that I was witnessing tangible evidence of a spiritual truth: As these people shaped and pounded and carved, they were hammering into existence buried images that revealed the soul, which seeks and learns of itself in concrete images.

As Keats recognized, for the soul to awaken, it must participate in earthly existence and is found in "reflections," much as Narcissus discovers himself by gazing into a pool. In this case, the pool was the work of art, the soul's artifact.

The necessity to acknowledge that we have a soul becomes more pressing as we age. As Ulanov points out, we become less and less concerned with worldly "success" and the endless demands the external world places upon us. She goes on to say that "these things are not what matter, but that something less perishable, more irreplaceable matters: the uniqueness of each human person. Christian faith talks about this as the life of the soul, the soul that lives outside of time and continues after time comes to an end. This, the soul's life, provides the terms of the end-questions."

The soul's life—its mysteries and complexities—continues to engage me as I pursue aging's meaning. In the process, I'm becoming more conscious of a cosmic dimension, the area into which my elephant's trunk gropes as it winds around the stone, dissolving into ripples that suggest a celestial sea. The trunk seems to be both searching the beyond and acting as an umbilical cord that unites me with it.

I'm reminded of the apostle Paul's saying, "Therefore we do not lose heart. Though outwardly we are wasting away, yet inwardly we are being renewed day by day." (2 Cor 4:16, NIV) As I become more aware of the truth of Paul's observation, I find myself looking at others more curiously, examining the lines and interesting textures their aging has produced. Instead of finding these results ugly or undesirable, I'm seeing the skin as a garment that alters through life and the body as a casing that will one day be transformed, not into a youthful ageless form, but one that will transcend all such terms.

Meanwhile, how do we live with our aging selves without despairing over the deterioration we see? I turn to Ulanov again: "Aging brings home to us what we have done or failed to do with our lives, our creativity or our waste, our openness to or zealous hiding from what really matters. Precisely at that point, age cracks us open, sometimes for the first time, makes us aware of the center, makes us look for it and for relation to it. Aging does not mark an end but rather the beginning of making sense of the end-questions, so that life can have an end in every sense of the word."

This cracking open that Ulanov describes also happens in the sculpting process, and I've observed that this action captures what I'm trying to articulate. In preparation for pouring bronze statues, the sculptor first makes a mold out of wax. Over the wax mold, she pours a casing that reminds me of human flesh in the way it conceals its treasure. Later the artist melts the wax, the outer casing sustaining the statue's shape for when the bronze is poured. Then white-hot liquid bronze fills the space where the wax once was, and when cooled, the sculptor chips off the casing, revealing the wondrous thing inside.

To me, chipping away the casing seems analogous to the way aging chips away at us. As Ulanov has pointed out and as Paul did before her, we shed the body, the outer self, when we die. And as the years pass, we become more frail and limited. Still, given the right circumstances, the inner life can become deeper and sharper, something of what I've been attempting to capture in these pages as I dream myself into old age. We can develop and bring to the surface hidden riches that compensate for our losses. However, for these inner changes to occur, we need to consciously engage life and not fall into the traps of despair and hopelessness and cynicism. Ulanov puts it this way: "If we spend a lifetime avoiding who we are, veering off from the central issues of finding and building our personal way of being, our personal ways of putting ourselves into the world...we reap the results in old age. We survive as unique persons who go on growing, experiencing, changing, and consolidating ourselves. Life continues to offer excitement." It is possible, then, to harvest a life lived fully right up until the end and to make fresh discoveries if we are open to new possibilities.

Florida Scott-Maxwell, author of *The Measure of My Days: One Woman's Vivid, Enduring Celebration of Life and Aging*, became a Jungian analyst at the age of fifty and is a model of someone who lived vigorously into old age. At eighty-two she wrote in her journal: "Age puzzles me. I thought it was a quiet time. My seventies were interesting, and fairly serene, but my eighties are passionate. I grow more intense as I age. To my own surprise I burst out with hot conviction. Only a few years ago I enjoyed tranquility, now I am so disturbed by the outer world and by human quality in general, that I want to put things right as though I still owed a debt to life. I must calm down. I am far too frail to indulge in moral fervor."[15]

Has aging a meaning? Like so many other things in life, it has the meaning we are willing to seek and bring to it. Contained within the aging process itself, as within a stone or a piece of clay, resides the meaning. But developing the life of the soul requires daring, the willingness to turn inward and chip away even when it grows tedious. In the process, perhaps our question will be answered.

TWENTY-SIX

THE TERM MAGIC IMPLIES SLEIGHT OF HAND, AN ABILITY TO make things appear and disappear at will. In a magic show, magicians exercise their ability to draw viewers' attention away from what the magicians are doing so they can convince those watching that a rabbit really does appear at random out of an empty hat or that any number of equally fantastic events can occur. In this case, the magic isn't magical in the sense of a supernatural intervention because there's a trick at its foundation. It involves the magician's skill at keeping the audience distracted enough not to notice the hoax involved.

Something similar happens with most artists. In the middle of a downtown street, a woman wearing red forms a focus—an apex—in a picture of shifting motion, a crowd moving, other buildings overlaid on the original scene. But the woman is constant, her red outfit standing out. Seeing with the camera lens has freed photographer Harry Callahan, opened him to what the human eye has been conditioned not to see—the multiplicity of life, the layers and levels of reality, from the everyday to the non-ordinary.

With a wide-angle lens, he expands the scene, extends its limits, and creates new relationships between objects, frequently using double or triple exposures. In a photo of a beach scene shot straight—without the collage/montage effect of super-imposed images—individuals in the water and on shore take on a new vulnerability. Reduced in size and stripped of their human superiority, we now see them more as part of nature than apart, dwarfed in relationship to the ocean's vastness and surrounding sand. They are caught in a new light, between our expectations of human importance and a world where size, power, and status mean little. Callahan has worked his magic on us.

Another artist, Jill Giegerich, combines collage, painting, and relief in her work. She introduces objects like wooden table legs that are the things themselves, and they also become something else in relationship to the new context. The surfaces she uses are not the usual rectangles or squares. Instead, they follow the curves and angles of the contents, the shapes not just a frame but part of the art itself. Within the plane of a piece, Giegerich creates illusions of different depths and dimensions, all happening simultaneously, giving a disquieting effect—sleight of hand at its most effective.

In photography, the camera lens "sees" something via the artist (or vice versa), records what it sees, and frames it. The camera is the grammar, the organizing principal that allows the artist's perceptions to be communicated to others.

In painting, the colors have meaning apart from the subject. They aren't dependent on an image to communicate emotions or ideas. The artist's lexicon is the palate, and nothing limits the range of colors/emotions that can be produced on a canvas. How colors react to each other and make new colors when mixed are the criteria. No longer does blue represent sky or water; it can become something new. Greens, too, may leap out of their assumed connection with nature and express something different. What a magic show this is!

While we don't let go entirely of the usual associations—and couldn't if we wanted to because they often are archetypal images and patterns that repeat themselves throughout history—we can entertain other possibilities. A sky can be green instead of blue; a lake can be red; a human purple. All of these colors, then, express a different perception of the thing perceived and strike the viewer freshly. They come in a side door and catch us off guard, triggering an emotional response that lifts us into a new awareness of ourselves and the environment.

By contrast, in writing, we are dependent on words and their multiple meanings to convey either a single idea or to suggest many interpretations. But words don't come directly from the head of Zeus. Instead they travel through the entire human social body, from the beginning of time, on the way picking up nuances, cultural inflections, meanings associated with a particular era. In short, they have baggage that both enriches and restricts, enhances and confuses. And that baggage continues to resonate today, just as our ancestors' idiosyncratic behaviors and histories plague later generations.

The word "nice" illustrates my meaning. According to the *Oxford*

English Dictionary, in the thirteenth and fourteenth centuries and as late as 1587, nice meant wanton, loose-mannered, and lascivious. Other meanings accrued to nice during that period, including foolish, stupid, senseless, strange, rare, uncommon, slothful, and lazy. By the end of the sixteenth century and on into the seventeenth, nice began to take on some of its current characteristics: nice meant to be coy, shy, modest, reserved, tactful, fastidious, dainty, and so on. Today, well, to be nice is not necessarily nice. It has become a bland, overused word with an imprecise meaning.

The other difficulty—or freedom—of language is the rules that accompany it. While singular words have resonance, it takes a string of words linked together by agreed-upon syntax and grammar to evoke larger meanings and complex thoughts. "Ape" gives me only a fuzzy picture of an ape, my personal image of ape. "Ape loping" causes me to see the animal in action. "Ape loping toward me" sets me in motion too.

Writers capture our attention through assembling strings of words that become a compelling narrative. Just as viewers at a magic show set aside their momentary doubts about what's happening before their eyes, so, too, do readers enter the narrative dream. That enables the writer to convince readers that the setting, characters, and events taking place are actually happening in real time when, in truth, they aren't. They only come to life in the readers' imaginations as they let go of their immediate world to undertake this journey into the unknown. Put this way, reading can seem like a potentially dangerous endeavor, and it can be if a writer's ideas and images shatter some preconceived notion about the world and about us.

Magic also can temporarily take people out of the constraints of everyday life and make them feel they can transcend it. Instead of being locked inside the usual routines that structure our days, we find release when something magical happens, such as when we watch a play in a theater and suddenly our world is transformed. We're no longer our daily selves, but we begin to identify with what's occurring on the stage, becoming a part of all the characters involved, good guys and bad guys.

Woody Allen's *Purple Rose of Cairo* is an example of this dynamic. An unhappily married Depression-era waitress played by Mia Farrow tries to escape her dull marriage by visiting picture shows and becomes transfixed with the movie *The Purple Rose of Cairo* and its lead character, archeologist Tom Baxter. When Tom literally steps off the screen and into her life, both realities are thrown into chaos. As happens with Mia's character, we're under the actors' and director's spell, convinced that the action unfolding in front of us is real, though it's only make-believe. It's as if the characters can step from the screen and interact with us.

It's easy to take the next step and see that most writing, whether a poem, a novel, or a play, has a magical component to it. The primary storytelling goal is magic, achieved by mysterious means. Words themselves are transformative in that they can so easily metamorphose into other words: "world" contains "word" and "old." Add or subtract a letter here or there and we've landed in a different meaning. Words in themselves are slippery and magical, calling forth images just by naming things: red chair, oak table, 2006 Honda Accord, green plaid coat, eucalyptus tree. Read the text and suddenly something appears in our mind's eye. Amazing!

And then there's the way the wind can blow open a door, filling the house with a gust of cold air, or the sun can illuminate a field and immediately transform our experience of that place. Or the timer on our living room lamp switches on silently and the room is now swathed in light, creating a totally different atmosphere. That's one reason we talk about something magical happening or of a place as being magical. In fact, the world is magical not only in its inherent changeability but also because of our interaction with it.

That's where realism enters the discussion. Reality is both magical and real, if by real we mean something that isn't imagined. I'm not a philosopher, but this computer I'm typing on has a life distinct from mine. My husband, who is sitting reading in a chair across from me, can see it and agree on its reality. But it also exists in a world where objects can become symbols for something else. So while my computer retains its identify as a writer's tool, it also can represent a window into another universe. It can become a metaphor for many things, just as most objects can.

This, then, seems to be the foundation for what we call magic realism. Language by its very nature is magical, transforming our everyday reality in multiple ways, carrying us aloft on the wings of thought. The writer confronts reality and tries to untangle it, to discover what is mysterious in things, in life, in human acts. The principle thing is not the creation of imaginary beings or worlds but the discovery of the mysterious relationship between our circumstances and us. The magical realist does not try to copy the surrounding reality but to seize the mystery that breathes behind things.

These observations deserve more explication. Magical realism isn't the only way art, and in this instance literature, reveals truths that otherwise might not be recognizable. Most literary writers are trying to understand in a more profound way the dynamics between individuals and groups. They're probing everyday events for what might be hidden from view. It isn't unlike what Don DeLillo's character Artis in *Zero K* observes: "I'm aware that when we see something, we are getting only a measure of information, a sense, an inkling of what really is there to see. I don't know the details or the terminology but I do know that the optic nerve is not telling the full truth. We're seeing only intimations. The rest is our invention, our way of reconstructing what is actual, if there is any such thing, philosophically, as what we call actual."

Artis could be speaking for the writer/artist who knows that our ordinary vision, our way of apprehending the world and its contents, is limited. Probing the actual, then, is what writers, as well as many visual artists, attempt. I'm thinking of Anthony Marra's collection of linked short stories *The Tsar of Love and Techno*. By taking his readers inside the fractured world of Chechnya and the former USSR between the 1930s, the present, and even beyond, he reveals the tragic consequences of Stalinist Russia and surroundings. In the book, art both reveals and conceals, as when a painter from the first story is forced to censor photographs and paintings. He airbrushes a ballerina out of a photograph, changes other pictures to make Stalin look better, and obliterates his brother's face from a family photo because his brother's religious beliefs made him a traitor in the harsh environment of the communist regime. Yet he later paints his brother's face in the background of every painting he is charged with altering.

This action demonstrates the power artists have, whether writers or visual artists, to alter what we call reality or the actual. What we think we are perceiving can suddenly shift. We easily can be deluded into believing what is being presented visually when there is little basis for its veracity. Donald Trump is an expert at creating this type of illusion by using his experience in so-called reality TV shows. But, aside from Trump's sleight of hand, we are constantly struggling to strip away the veils that obscure our understanding of things in the hope we'll come closer to whatever reality is.

Writers who employ magical realism have a unique method. They don't try to delude the reader into thinking what is presented on the page is real in the sense it is something that could actually happen. Instead, the narrative leans more in the opposite direction, presenting images and descriptions that the reader understands are not true to our lived life but still contain an even more persuasive reality.

This approach isn't new. In reading about Virgil's *Aeneid* in Richard Jenkyns's *Classical Literature*, I came across the following: "Virgil makes the familiar become strange: the Trojans see the River Tiber breaking out into the sea from thick forest, after having sailed past the scented and mysterious island of the enchantress Circe by night, hearing her song and the howling of her animals. Tiber is miraculously stilled before Aeneas travels up it to Evander's town on the site of future Rome; the trees and waters marvel, as though they had come alive, and the boat cuts through the woodland as though penetrating a jungle."

First, the Tiber is actually in Rome, but in this narrative, the river is linked to Circe's island, a fictional world. Next, this powerful river is temporarily at rest to allow Aeneas to safely reach Evander's town. Then, the trees and waters are anthropomorphized, responding emotionally to what has just happened. Finally, this vessel created to travel in water also can move on land and in a thickly wooded area. Virgil isn't trying to convince his readers that these things are true to our lived life, but he is showing that those things we take for granted can step out of character and behave differently, contradicting our expectations. His descriptions demonstrate the mystery underlying the Trojan's journey. A study would show, I'm sure, that many other texts inhabit the magical realism genre if not fully then partially.

This passage reminds me of what quantum mechanics suggests about our universe. Some physicists believe that many interacting worlds—known as MIW—exist in vast numbers, are real, and "exert influence on each other." Further:

There are three main points to the MIW theory . . . First, that the universe we live in is just one of an unknown 'gigantic' number of worlds, some of which are 'almost identical to ours,' but most are 'very different.' Second, all of the worlds are 'equally real,' existing continuously through time with precisely defined properties. Third, quantum phenomena arise from 'a universal force of repulsion between 'nearby' (i.e. similar) worlds, which tends to make them more dissimilar.' 'All quantum effects arise from, and only from, the interaction between worlds,' the physicists explained in their abstract.[16]

I'm not a physicist, but as a writer I can speculate about this theory. Since everything that could have happened in our past but did not has occurred in the past of some other universe, time may not necessarily always follow its prescribed linear path or could be much more complicated than what we believe. The MIW theory also opens the possibility that humans will be able to interact one day with some of these parallel worlds. We could conclude that in its way, magical realism is more real than naturalistic, representational fiction.

TWENTY-SEVEN

WHENEVER I GIVE READINGS OF MY NOVELS, THE MAIN question I'm asked is "Where did the story come from?" or "Why did you write it?" Many authors use past incidents as a springboard and friends and family members as models for the characters they create, as I did in my novels *Fling!* and *Freefall: A Divine Comedy.* When I teach creative writing, I talk about ways to use individuals from our past (or present) as skeletons that can be fleshed out as full-bodied characters. But there are numerous occasions when a work's origins can't be located in a writer's past, at least not on a surface level. Even if our characters do start out with a tie to someone we've known, usually the story takes over and those earlier experiences fall away, allowing the writer to clothe her creations so they are unrecognizable by the original person.

My second published novel began in a drastically different way. It demonstrated that a narrative's origin can be mysterious, the seeds often germinating for years before finally surfacing. This was the case with *Curva Peligrosa*, released by Regal House Publishing in September 2017. The story first took hold of me in 2000. Here is what I wrote in my writer's journal on July 16, 2000, though I didn't actually start writing the book until 2003:

> Was taken with the image of the tornado that swept into Pine Lake, a resort near Red Deer, Alberta, yesterday, not far from where I was born. It has killed several people, flattening trailers, etc. It isn't the destruction that interests me. It's devastating and unimaginable. It's the tornado's image, the swirling dark funnel that seems to connect both sky and earth, so blameless in itself, just doing what tornadoes do.

The tornado has a magical, mythical quality, similar to the earthquake that set Dorothy off on her adventures in *The Wizard of Oz*. And it's an image I can imagine using to start a book or story. There's something in it for me, the way it gathers up so much in one swoop and then sets everything down in a new place, reconfigured. This is what interests me, and I don't know what to do with it, but it has a compelling quality. It's gripped my imagination. It's odd how these things happen. The force they have. Novelists and writers in general are like tornados themselves in how they rearrange lives, facts, and places.

Not surprisingly, the novel opens with a tornado that sweeps through the fictional town of Weed, Alberta, and drops a purple outhouse into its center. Drowsing and dreaming inside that structure is its owner, Curva Peligrosa, a curiosity and a marvel, a source of light and heat, a magnet. Adventurous, amorous, fecund, and over six feet tall, she also possesses magical powers.

Where on earth did this character come from? That question still pursues me, even though I've completed the book and it is out in the world. How did its beginnings in a newspaper article get translated into a full-length work that doesn't have any visible connections to people I've known except peripherally?

My interest in Jung's ideas surfaces again here. I see archetypal elements in this work, especially in its main character, Curva Peligrosa. Not surprisingly, Curva didn't fully come alive for me until I discovered her name. Originally, I had called her Lupita, yet I was having trouble grasping Lupita's personality. She wasn't gaining traction on the page or in my imagination.

But then my husband and I visited Cuernavaca, a small town a two-hour drive from Mexico City. As the driver took us to our destination, I kept seeing signs along the roadside with the words *curva peligrosa*, which means dangerous curve. The name itself released this character. Suddenly, I could hear her speak, I could see her interacting with others, and I knew her—the lustiness, the gravelly voice, the larger-than-life aspect. She seemed to emerge full blown as Athena did from Zeus's head, and Curva also has a mythical quality.

This fantastical dimension seems evident from the moment Curva rides her horse into Weed, a goat following close behind. With her glittering gold tooth that glints whenever she smiles, she is a vision from a surrealistic western, wearing turquoise rings, a serape, and a flat-brimmed black hat. A parrot perched on each shoulder and carrying a couple of six-shooters as well as a rifle after a twenty-year trek up the Old North Trail from southern Mexico, she is ready to settle down. But are the inhabitants of Weed ready for her? With an insatiable appetite for life and love, Curva's infectious energy impacts the townspeople. She has the greenest of thumbs, creating a tropical habitat in an arctic clime, and she possesses a wicked trigger finger, her rifle and six-shooters never far away.

Curva's larger-than-life presence challenges the residents of Weed, who have never seen anything like her, and, I must admit, I hadn't either. I am neither six feet tall nor as buxom as Curva. In general, I'm pretty conventional and have never backpacked or traveled hundreds of miles by horse with a travois. Where did this woman come from? Clearly, she had resided somewhere in my depths, so far away that I hadn't discovered her previously.

A kind of shadow figure, unlike me, Curva is amoral and not bound by the usual codes and limited choices that restrict many middle-class women. She lives fully in her senses, bedding with multiple men if she desires, enjoying what she refers to as walking marriages where a woman invites a man to spend a sweet night with her, but he must leave by daybreak. She also pursues her dreams, no matter what hardships she encounters in doing so, such as trekking the Old North Trail off and on for twenty years with only animals for companions.

A participant in the 1960s second-wave feminism, it's no wonder I gave birth to a powerful female character like Curva since my options early in life were severely limited. I had a son to raise on my own and received no child support from his father. A quick learner, I parlayed the typing skills I had studied in my high school commercial course into a variety of office jobs. Consequently, in Curva Peligrosa, I created a female character who is fully feminine but not as restricted as I had been either by self-imposed limits or by society's boundaries. I also wanted to create someone who was unlike most women I know.

While Curva may not resemble most females, she does reflect elements of various goddesses. Her love of nature and willingness to travel alone in the wilderness reminds me of Artemis, goddess of the hunt. She also can be associated with a kind of Eve figure who creates her own Garden of Eden in Weed, wanting the northerners to experience this more idyllic state that her lush greenhouse represents. And like Eve, she sets up conflicts in the Weedites after making them aware of possibilities beyond their limited vision. Finally, Curva is an earthmother. She's a kind of Demeter figure, associated with animals and the earth, and doesn't do well in chronological time.

Curva Peligrosa doesn't have any obvious autobiographical roots, but the narrative does have some parallels to historical moments in the province of Alberta. When I was growing up in that part of western Canada, agriculture was the main source of income. But in 1947, significant oil reserves were discovered at Leduc, Alberta, ushering in the oil boom that continues today. It brought job seekers and others to the area, eager to exploit the province's riches.

I must have registered these developments subliminally, even though it wasn't something I was particularly conscious of at the time. As a young woman, I did secretarial work for Sinclair Canada Oil and other American petroleum companies. Impressionable, I thought the Texas accents signified power and prosperity and wanted to emulate them, faking a drawl whenever I could. It took me awhile to realize that, in fact, Americans were taking over our land and much of its oil.

My association with these southerners fueled my interest in moving to America in my early twenties. Eventually, I became an American citizen so that, as a single parent, I could take advantage of California's low-tuition state university system and earn degrees. You could say that the exploitation was then mutual. I didn't discover oil, but I did find its intellectual equivalent: higher education that I couldn't have gotten in Canada at the time. However, the earlier image of American oilmen making off with our prairie identity stayed with me, surfacing in Curva Peligrosa and in Curva's concerns over what she was witnessing in Weed. But none of this was intentional when I began the narrative. I had no idea then where it would take me.

In the novel, Shirley, an Americano who is buying up nearby land so he can own all of the oil rights, represents the kind of southerner from my earlier experience of working for American petroleum companies. In *Curva Peligrosa*, he ends up being a villain in the old sense of the word, and many readers will end up hissing at him. In turn, Shirley seems to embrace that identity, enjoying the turmoil he is creating not only in Curva but also in the Weedites themselves. (I had created a kind of Trumpian character long before Trump started causing chaos in America.)

Like Curva, while I'm not adverse to some kinds of development, I do recognize that the word itself can be misleading. In certain cases, development might represent economic growth and prosperity for the people involved. For example, the Blackfoot tribe in *Curva Peligrosa* benefits from the oil wealth. It allows them to build a museum that highlights Native life and to open their own university. Under the leadership of their chief Billie One Eye, the wealth gives them an identity they otherwise had lacked, even though they sold out to the Americano in order to enrich themselves. Billie acts as a bridge to the Native world that has a closer connection to nature and the mainstream life of the Weedites. He's an artist and being blind in one eye has caused him to see more clearly. An embodiment of tribal wisdom who counters some of Curva's excesses, he's practical, grounded, and credible.

Yet in many other instances, such development can deplete the land of valuable resources and drastically disturb the environment, improving a few lives but enslaving others. This becomes one of Curva's concerns. She also hates how life's pace has speeded up, not leaving time for the basics, such as enjoying leisurely meals with friends and loved ones, fiestas, and sex.

I hadn't set out to write a novel that had a political slant, but once I became involved in Curva's quest, I didn't have any choice but to follow along and express her concerns. In the process, I learned how seeds planted in our unconscious early on can sprout and bloom in our writing. Historically, the novel shows the way American dominance has infected parts of Canada. It has overshadowed the Canadian ethos of equality for all, respect for the environment, desire for safety and peace and politeness. It also has dramatized its notions of progress that ignored the exploitation of the natural world. Shirley, who attracts Curva more than she wants to admit, resembles a sky god and the *puer aeternus,* used in mythology to designate a child-god who is forever young; psychologically it can refer to an older man whose emotional life has remained at an adolescent level. Shirley lives more in the stratosphere, unconnected to the emotional life of others.

But there's another aspect to Curva that I haven't mentioned. In reading Gareth Hill's book *Masculine and Feminine: The Natural Flow of Opposites in the Psyche,* I came across his ideas of psychic energy being divided into four quadrants or principles: the static feminine, the dynamic feminine, the dynamic masculine, and the static masculine. After reading Hill's book, I discovered Curva's possible roots in my psyche. I had been discussing Hill's ideas with Dr. Y and felt that Curva fits into the dynamic feminine category. She has similar qualities to what Hill describes: "The dynamic feminine is the synthesizing creation of new possibilities and new combinations. It is the insight, awareness, gnosis, that comes only through actual experience. Its effects are the uplifting, ecstatic inspiration that comes from the experience of transformed awareness." This aspect of the feminine is closely associated with Dionysus, the dancing maenad, and the trickster—all elements in Curva's personality.

Dr. Y and I had also explored the notion that when I'm writing fiction, I'm using a form of "active imagination," a practice that Jung endorsed, as I create and engage these characters that emerge from my psyche. It had occurred to me that the dynamic feminine, as Hill describes that force, had been suppressed in me. Curva isn't afraid of standing up to the masculine and even taking on a male identity for periods of time when she needs to make money riding broncos at rodeos in the 1940s and 50s. Sometimes a woman needs to masquerade as a male to succeed or to develop her skills, as Curva does in the novel when she pretends to be her dead twin brother, Xavier, and as so many other women across the world have done— and continue to do—today.

Choosing Curva Peligrosa for her name connects her to the shadowy world of my unconscious. She is also someone who can throw dangerous curves and isn't likely to be welcomed by the more conscious side of my personality. If I had let her loose when I was a younger woman and lived out her behavior, I would have been going against societal norms, making it much more difficult to raise my son—and myself! Curva also is dangerous in the sense that she has otherworldly, "witchlike" qualities that prejudiced men and some women like to attack.

Dr. Y wondered if my novels were an expression of a side of myself that I couldn't have lived out as a single mother. Doing so would have created major problems for me and my son. Women who ignore social constraints create a lot of turmoil for themselves and others. And in naming her, I'm also relegating Curva to the more shadowy world of my unconscious. This led me to realize that by claiming Curva is nothing like me, her creator, I might be protesting too much. Dr. Y wondered if *Curva Peligrosa* might not be the autobiography of my shadow, in Jungian terms those qualities, impulses, and emotions that we cannot bear for others to see and thus hide. By fictionalizing this part of myself, I don't get thrown in jail and involved in dangerous experiences with men.

I've now come to see that Curva can be read on many levels. She can be seen literally as being an Hispanic woman who breaks free of a strongly patriarchal society where most of the people adhere to the church's teachings. She makes her own moral code. She also can be viewed symbolically as a stand in for the kind of woman who can set out on her own, equal to a male in the same circumstances. And she can be viewed as a psychological representative of a woman who moves from the southern hemisphere, often associated with a more matriarchal perspective, as well as the unconscious, to the northern more patriarchal sphere. What she accomplishes is much of the novel's dramatic excitement.

When Curva Peligrosa made her way into the publishing world in 2017, not only did Curva leave behind the Old North Trail and her creator, but she also stepped into her readers' imaginations and, I hope, continues to plant seeds that could grow for some time, allowing her creative explorations to endure.

POETRY

TWENTY-EIGHT

A S A POET, I'VE ALWAYS FELT POETRY'S TREMENDOUS importance. It stimulates our imaginations and tunes up a part of our thought processes that keep us open to new ideas. Perhaps more important, poetry connects us to our deeper selves. Still, I can get caught up in the complexities of modern life: I have classes to prepare for, student papers to read, several writing projects demanding attention, a household to care for. It's easy to forget that poetry is as necessary to our emotional well-being as food.

When I was teaching undergraduates and told them of poetry's many virtues, most of them said they had trouble reading poems. "Why," I asked, "in a class of twenty literate, intelligent young men and women do only two or three read or write poetry—even occasionally?"

They thought about the question, and then a few raised their hands tentatively; they tried to articulate why poetry was hard for them: "It doesn't have anything to do with my life," said a female business major from Hong Kong. "I can't get it," said a male psychology major from Philadelphia. "I feel silly saying I read poetry; people think you're weird if you do," admitted another young woman from Los Angeles. "They're too depressing; they always seem to be about sad things," claimed someone else.

I urged them to give poetry a chance, reminding them that poems compress the use of language, so they work like instant food: you need to add water before eating it. With poetry, instead of water, you need to bring your full attention, mind, imagination, and heart. If you do, the poem will open and reveal itself to you. And so will most dreams.

In the following passage, the poet William Stafford tells us how to read a poem:

Poetry is the kind of thing you have to see from the corner of your eye . . . It's like a very faint star. If you look straight at it, you can't see it, but if you look a little to one side it is there . . . If you analyze it away, it's gone. It would be like boiling a watch to find out what makes it tick. If you let your thoughts play, turn things this way and that, be ready for liveliness, alternatives, new views, the possibility of another world—you are in the area of poetry.[17]

Teaching poetry reminds me that while we dream and write poetry in solitude, to fully engage a poem is a communal activity. Similarly, to apprehend a dream, it helps to discuss it with someone—a friend, a therapist. While I might sit down alone with a poem and enter into the poet's world, with a group something magical happens. Connections I hadn't thought of spring to life; observations that hadn't occurred to me add a whole new dimension to the poem. I'm reminded that something similar happens at a good poetry reading. Perhaps hearing the poem with other interested individuals triggers neurons in our brains that otherwise might not have been touched.

But I still hadn't convinced my students that poetry was accessible and important. One student blurted out, "They're too deep. They're frightening!" This response captures, I think, much of what we fear in poetry: It carries us past safe waters; there's no lifeguard on duty; we can get in over our heads quickly, taken out to sea. We can discover new territories in ourselves—uncharted, savage, uninhabitable.

By now my students are somewhat dazed. Nothing quiets or humbles them quite like poetry. They stare at their books and then at me, mouths open, eyes a bit glassy, trying to understand. I tell them not to worry so much about understanding: "You need to enter the poem, but also let the poem enter you, penetrate you, plant its seeds, carry you away on the wings of imagination. Let it touch deep chords that will reverberate long after you've finished reading the poem."

TWENTY-NINE

WHEN I ENTERED THE MASTER'S IN CREATIVE WRITING program at San Francisco State University several years ago, I discovered the work being done by poets I'd not read carefully before—many of them women, work that was more innovative than I'd been used to. This writing didn't fit into the genre of lyric poetry as I understood it. It was largely autobiographical material, snapshots of these writers' pasts focusing on particular emotional content, ending with an epiphany, a "point."

I had learned that lyrical poets were supposed to use autobiography, memories of experienced events, whether real or imagined, to carry larger ideas about human nature, time, the universe. (I recognize that in a certain way all poetry is autobiographical. We're charting the geography of our psyche as projected into language/objects/ images.)

The more experimental poets—Kathleen Fraser, Michael Palmer, Susan Howe, Norma Cole, Leslie Scalapino, Lyn Hejinian, Stephen Ratcliffe, to name a few—use the page and language differently, literally voyaging into unexplored territory in the way they place words on the page and break lines. The music and "thinking" of their poetry make something happen on the page, treating it as theater, letting meanings emerge from this dynamic rather than re-creating a remembered event. They push language to its limits, attempting to bring into the poem a larger world by shattering syntax, rethinking grammar, challenging the notions of narrative as we know it, pushing beyond linear cause-and-effect thinking into new realms. They are questioning the very fabric of our daily life, the notions of subject and subjectivity, of art and its role in our culture.

Not that there's anything wrong with our usual way of perceiving through language and its rules; many complex, mysterious things can be conveyed in traditional ways. But as Orwell pointed out in his essay "Politics and the English Language,"[18] clichés and hackneyed images prevent us from being discerning and distort rather than reveal. So, too, can our usual ways of speaking and writing prevent us from experiencing a multi-dimensional, fragmented, chaotic, bizarre, inexpressible reality, often with an organizing center that may be different from what we expect.

A poem that illustrates these ideas is one by Kathleen Fraser, formerly with San Francisco State's Creative Writing Department, cofounder of the innovative literary magazine *How(ever)* (now out of print) and publisher of several poetry collections. The following poem is from *Something (Even Human Voices) in the Foreground, a Lake*.

They Did Not Make Conversation

A lake as big, the early evening wind at the bather's neck. Something pulling (or was it rising up) green from the bottom. You could lie flat and let go of the white creases. You could indulge your fear of drowning in the arms of shallow wet miles. You did not open your mouth, yet water poured into openings, making you part. Bone in the throat. That dark blue fading, thinning at the edges. On deck chairs with bits of flowered cloth across their genitals, the guests called out in three languages and sometimes pointed, commenting on the simple beauty of bought connection. The swan-like whiteness of the day. That neck of waves. There was always a tray with small red bottles. And pin-pointed attentions, at each slung ease.

In this poem, Fraser accomplishes what she articulates in the flyleaf to her book *Notes Preceding Trust*: "I wish, in my work, to resist habit (mine and others'), to uncover something fresh that connects with the reader in a way she or he could not have predicted. An ache, a splash of cold water, a recognition."

In the poem's opening, we are presented with "a lake as big." The immediate impulse is to ask "as big as what?" But if we resist that impulse, we discover the comparison is more powerful by having it open-ended. Our imaginations are left to fill in the blank.

Another reading would be to compare the lake to the early evening wind, which extends the comparison to something invisible but tangible. This lake, then, isn't an actual lake. It takes on mythic, magical proportions—suggesting perhaps the waters of the unconscious, unfathomable and illimitable.

In the next group of words, the speaker questions her own perceptions of "something pulling . . . green from the bottom." There are various ways to read this phrase. We either can see it as something actually pulling the color green from the bottom, bringing it into view, perhaps the bather. Or we can hear it as something green—fresh, new, living—that is pulling (rising up) from the bottom on its own.

Then the reader is brought in, the first complete sentence, the previous phrases like the breath that precedes a spoken thought, rising up green from the bottom. We are part of the poem's setting. It's now possible to let go of the "white creases," which could be the lighter indentations that are left in folds of skin when we are out in the sun for a long time, those vulnerable spots hidden from glaring rays. But they also could be the crease in a page, perhaps where a book folds at its center. Maybe the "you" is a book/page—or, put another way, you are compared to a book/page—that can open up, let go, "indulge your fear of drowning in the arms of shallow wet miles."

And we do fear drowning, especially in shallow water: what could be more humiliating than to drown in water that isn't over our heads? Yet our fears often are just as groundless. However, the provocative part of this image is the "wet miles." Again, we don't know what the miles encompass, giving the image more suggestiveness. The ambiguity causes our hidden fears of the unknown to surface and we imagine an endless expanse of miles, wet now from the lake that the poem grows out of.

As the title suggests, this poem is about—among other things—our inability to communicate and connect with others, except at times via "bought connection." And for me Fraser accomplishes what she hopes to do: she creates an ache, a splash of recognition. She takes me into that bleak landscape, the frightening dimension always present in human relations but rarely alluded to.

Just as the visual artist's purpose—one of them, at least—is to help us see beyond the accepted meanings, to shake up our perceptions, so writers, too, use their colors/words in new, unexpected ways. As Poet Elaine Equi says in *Mirage* No. 3 (The Women's Issue):

Experimental when it refers to literature is usually connected with the idea of avant-garde and/or the act of challenging traditional forms. To be an experimental writer implies rebellion, but I prefer to give the idea of experimentation its scientific connotation which is closer to a method of discovery.

Innovative writing stretches our perceptions, shows us things— even turns certain words into objects—in new, unexpected relationships, causes us to stop, to look. In doing so, we have expanded our vision—discovered that "these things aren't fancies, but facts."[19]

THIRTY

"Art does not reproduce what we see—it makes us see."
—Paul Klee

ONE GOAL THAT MY HUSBAND AND I HAVE ON OUR TRAVELS is to visit as many major art museums as possible. As I've already indicated, museums have become our way of accessing the sublime and finding inspiration. While visiting the Musée d'Orsay in Paris a few years ago, home of so many major impressionistic paintings, I copied Monet's words: "Try to forget what objects you have before you, a tree, a house, a field, or whatever. Merely think, here is a little square of blue, here an oblong of pink, here a streak of yellow, and paint it as it looks to you, the exact color and shape, until it gives your own impression of the scene before you." As a writer and neophyte in the visual arts, these words have encouraged me to trust in what I see, to push language— or whatever medium I'm using—until it renders external and internal reality in new ways, helping me to discover just what it is I'm perceiving.

Another way of describing this approach is "bare attention," the Buddhist meditation goal of eliminating projections and expectations of people and things until we draw closer to their essence. We need to remove all preconceived notions so we can apprehend the world anew each time we experience it. It's impossible to follow this principle exactly, but the closer we get, the more challenging our art becomes. We enter the heart of things (like "heart court"?) instead of just replicating familiar, agreed-upon surfaces, the writer as surprised by what she uncovers as the reader. Or to quote Frost, "No surprise for the writer, no surprise for the reader." Eleanor

Wilner gives another perspective: "What is troubling about too much of our poetry is that, without aesthetic distance, it remains in the realm of ego, of what we think we know, or what we want or think we ought to see."[20] Art loses something essential when it remains "in the realm of ego" and we avoid the unknown that can shock and awaken us.

Matisse also understood this problem. Jack Flam, reviewing a Matisse show in *The New York Review,* observes that "It is as if each time he [Matisse] approached a subject, even a familiar one, he was seeing it for the first time. Or, as he himself said, as if he were seeing 'with the eyes of a child.' The ideal that underlies this way of working goes directly back to impressionism, especially to Claude Monet's notion of the innocent eye."

I seek poets who possess this innocent eye, who fearlessly extend language and perception, shaking loose some new awareness. Each person has a perspective that can't be duplicated exactly: no one has quite the same experiences that we do. That's what I'm after when I read poetry: a unique way of seeing and experiencing the world.

Of course, many poets see in a fresh, challenging way. But Susan Howe, Gustaf Sobin, and Cole Swenson have a particular vision and style that I find intriguing. Howe began as a visual artist before she turned to poetry; her work shows this influence. She uses language at times as paint, splattering words onto the page, conscious of them as things in themselves (just as abstract painters see color and paint as a sufficient focus for a painting—the subject matter). Howe draws our attention at times to the surfaces of language, not just its layers of meaning and suggestiveness, revealing new universes of perception. She also uses the whole page as one would a canvas—the recognition of different planes intersecting as in a painting and an appreciation of foreground and background. This holds as much interest for her as the words themselves. Perhaps more often than most poets, Howe exploits the possibilities of placing words on a page, increasing the texture which she is incorporating into a poem.

In the stuttering title, "There are not leaves enough to crown to cover to crown to cover," the first section in her long poem *The Europe of Trusts,* Howe writes, "Life opens into conceptless perspectives. Language surrounds chaos." Many of her poems embody this idea, the language just barely containing the chaos on the page. Here's a section from "I. Pearl Harbor":

GHOST enters WAVES he
scatters flowers
from the summit
of a cliff that beckons on or beetles o'er
his base
ORISONS
wicket-gate
wicket-gate

MAGPIES clatter

1 2 3

and TALKATIVE
(Walks all this time by himself saying
he says to me softly—)
What.

The capitalized words (GHOST, WAVES, ORISONS, MAGPIES, and TALKATIVE) function as foreground, standing out from the other words and popping out at the reader, carrying more weight and emphasis. Calling attention to themselves, they alter the music of the poem, giving a much different beat than if they were all lower case. Instead of "ghost enters," which makes the emphasis equal in both words, we have GHOST enters, shifting the emphasis to ghost.

All of these words are nouns, though waves can cross borders and function as a verb, too (in either meaning, "wave" suggests motion), as it does in this instance. Read alone, the capitalized words almost make sense, forming their own poem within the poem. The ghost could either be THE famous ghost, perhaps Hamlet's dead father, or it also could be the ghost of the narrator's father, who was mentioned in the opening part of the book, or both.

At times, it's ambiguous as to what is happening in the poem. Clearly, the poet isn't trying to make conventional narrative sense, to tell a story in the usual way. Instead, she shakes up our notions of narrative and the sentence, letting many of the words fly by themselves, their relationship with the ones that precede or follow being uncertain or having multiple possibilities. Charles Bernstein puts it this way:

Not 'death' of the referent—rather a recharged use of the multivalent referential vectors that any word has, how words in combination tone and modify the associations made for each of them, how 'reference' then is not a one-on-one relation to an 'object' but a perceptual dimension that closes in to pinpoint, nail down (this word), sputters omnitropically (the in in the which of who where what wells), refuses the build up of image track/projection while, pointillistically, fixing a reference at each turn.[21]

"GHOST enters WAVES he" can be read in several ways. The ghost has entered the water/waves. Or the ghost enters and then waves at someone. Or the poet could just be sketching in a scene, like giving stage directions (in a way, the whole passage reads like stage directions to a drama of the mind): "GHOST enters. Waves." "He / scatters flowers / from the summit / of a cliff that beckons on or beetles o'er" could be referring to the ghost or to someone else. The referent isn't clear, and these words might be refusing "the buildup of image track/projection." (Of course, in a long poem, it's difficult to assume a meaning from just one portion of it.)

What is clear is the potential threat. We can't ignore the cliff that's beckoning, jutting out like a beetled brow. The ghost seems to merge with this cliff, scattering prayers like the flowers from the summit. Wicket gate sounds like "wicked gate," though it literally suggests a gate within a gate—and the sport cricket. I think the poet has more interest in the sounds of these words, of giving the impression of magpies chattering (three of them? 1 2 3). If you say "wicked gate" quickly several times and just hear the sounds, it resembles magpies chattering. And what does this gate open onto? Memory? The poet's well of associations? The gate between the living and the dead?

Where are we and who "is walking by himself saying / he says to me softly—) // What"? In the poem, "What" isn't a question; it's a statement. What comes up again on the next page, twice, framing the words "what a few fragments holds us to what" (the spacing on the page isn't so linearly narrative as I've shown here). Again, by Howe italicizing and positioning "what" in this way, the word's sound becomes more noticeable, as if these magpies have formed a chorus, "what" being the only utterance they know.

The lines I've quoted here seem to be fragments from a child's memory of the war. This part of the poem starts like a journal entry, Buffalo / 12.7.41, and conveys a specific memory: "(Late afternoon light.) / (Going to meet him in snow.) / HE / (Comes through the hall door.)"

As in a play, this chorus of magpies surveys the scene, the poet a magpie who is talkative, talkative, opening the wicket gate of memory and language that opens into another wicket gate, the writer giving us a fresh perspective on all of this. History. The impact of war on a child's imagination. Felt more deeply because it's referred to obliquely, the memory is almost a ghost of the original experience.

In a very different way, Gustaf Sobin—an American poet and author who lived in Provence for over forty years—mines the external world and, to a lesser degree, memory in the following poem:

The Cheval Glass

(T'ang)
glances back-
ward be-
tween the
two
turquoise flamingoes;
fingers
swim to her cheeks,
fork
through
those tossed fires . . .
my
shadows, too, drift
into the image, my
arms take
root
in her sleeves....
So

many cells for that
gray
glowing oval; her
pearls spill,

clicking,
be-
tween
its tapering beaks.

Sobin likes to inhabit the middle of a page in his poems. Many of them flare out from the center, suggesting a desire to claim the whole sheet rather than clinging to the left margin, as so many poems do. However, he exerts tight control over the words, marching them down the interior, unlike Howe's no-less-controlled placing but still a looser claim of the whole canvas through unconventional placements of the lines. In fact, this particular poem by Sobin resembles in shape the object of the title, cheval glass being a long mirror that is mounted in a frame so that it can be tilted.

Unlike standard mirrors that are fixed to walls, this one can shift its focus, taking in more or less, depending on its positioning. Here the poet/narrator behaves as the cheval glass, giving the viewer a skewed perspective on the contents of what appears to be a display case in a museum where he and a female companion are viewing two flamingoes from the T'ang dynasty, known for its encouragement and patronage of the arts, especially poetry and ceramics. Just as the poet's vision can shift, depending on his or her position, so too the contents of this glass case are altered by these two viewers and the narrator's description of what he's seeing.

It isn't clear who or what "glances back- / ward be- / tween the / two / turquoise flamingoes." It's tempting to read that "The Cheval Glass" does the glancing since the poet is careful to construct grammatically correct sentences, not sentence fragments, and "Cheval Glass" acts as the subject for what follows. If it is the cheval glass, then the mirror suggests how language mirrors consciousness and also conveys the past, a symbol of the poet trying to capture with words what essentially can't be captured. Mirrors reveal what is in front of them at the moment, but there are also lingering images of all previous reflections and perhaps future ones. Language and mirror merge into a metaphor.

In the poem, the viewer keeps getting mixed up in the thing viewed, as in the lines "fingers // swim to her cheeks, / fork / through / those tossed fires... / my // shadows, too, drift into the image." Not only is the narrator's companion fused now with the flamingo ceramics, but the narrator is part of what's being viewed and also gets ensnared in his companion's "sleeves," just as her "pearls spill, / clicking, // be- / tween / its tapering beaks." Similarly, it's impossible for a poet not to leave something of himself or herself in a poem or not to become entwined with the subject matter. Anything touched by language loses its purity and contaminates the other.

By breaking the two-syllable words "backward" and "between" at their spine, so to speak, Sobin mimics this disjunction he's narrating of the split in perception, calling attention to how the meanings of the words themselves change when the two parts cease to exist on the same line. They become heightened, emphasized, at the same time as they suggest an alternate meaning, "mirroring" what he's noticing in the reflections he describes in the poem. Something slips between the syllables, allowing in new connotations and perceptions that traditional narrative can keep out. Even the verbs "swim" and "fork" challenge our perceptions, giving off such opposite connotations, the image of fingers swimming to her cheeks creating a dreamy, unconscious gesture, countered in the next line by the more alert, direct, and swift movement of "fork." Perhaps the narrator is suggesting that to experience the image he's describing requires both states of mind, dreamy and attentive.

But a poet can write what resembles conventional narrative and still create the disruption I've been describing, as does Cole Swenson, who has published several poetry collections as well as translations from French works:

> "Work in Progress: Dusk,"
> Because there is a band playing
> in the park the people linger
> so their children keep on running,
> charcoal smudges going
> deeper into the paper
> disappearing into the fur
> of the dark and then
> emerging. Small druids
> in their bodies whenever
> their parents aren't watching.
> No, just smudges growing
> arms and running closer
> the way form spreads across canvas
> even while the painter is watching.

Something ominous looms over the seemingly innocent scene of families lingering to listen to a band playing in the park. We don't know what kind of band is playing; nor do we know what kind of music it's performing. It could be anything from a brass band with horns and drums doing time-honored songs like a Sousa march, to a rock or jazz group. The type of music doesn't seem to matter: the group becomes a temporary focal point for this scene, binding together the participants. Yet everything remains unspecific here—people, children, park, band, painter. We're floating in the amorphous world of the general noun, blobs of impressionistic color guiding us rather than clearly delineated forms, acting at a particular place and time. The wonderful and scary thing about such generality is that it isn't grounding; it isn't concrete. It forces us to work a little harder as readers and to remain with the uncertainty of not having a tangible situation to react to and with. We're kept outside the fences of language, the images "charcoal smudges going / deeper into the paper / disappearing into the fur / of the dark and then / emerging."

These lines speak to me of how a poem can work on us, the paper the poem is printed on like a vast forest and not just the individual tree that produced it, the page having depth and dimension that mirrors our depths. These words we rely on to convey meaning and imagery are elusive, penetrating the dark and at the same time extracting something that darkness contains—what we hope art will do. In this case, the children become "small druids / in their bodies whenever / their parents aren't watching." So for a moment the children shift shape, turning into these forces of nature that can lead us into a fuller appreciation of it.

Then they come into focus again, not just smudges, but "growing / arms and running closer." We can't hold onto the children any more than we can hold onto the meaning of these words that penetrate the paper and our minds, everything being elusive, out of our control, "the way form spreads across canvas / even while the painter is watching." We're helpless to do much more than apprehend, recognizing that anything we try to contain in art or nature will escape our clutches, a reminder that it isn't only the more "experimental" poets who challenge our perceptions and shake up our expectations, though Cole Swenson's body of work leans more toward the innovative than the conventional.

The poems I've discussed here embody multiple truths, multiple approaches to language, multiple ways of seeing. These poets subvert our usual perceptions, forcing us to view poetry, the world, and ourselves freshly. But the reader also needs an innocent eye and a willingness to embrace many perspectives. Then these poems can fully convey their mysteries.

THIRTY-ONE

I'VE READ AN ARTICLE ON JAMES JOYCE IN THE NEW YORKER
that has blown my mind. I finally better understand what I've
been trying to do in my more experimental poetry. In discussing
Finnegans Wake, Louis Menand tells us,

> *Finnegans Wake* is not a prose poem, which is probably how
> many people would like to read it. It's a work of realist fiction.
> It's just that the reality it represents is nighttime reality, the
> dream life, which Joyce believed required the invention of
> a new mode of language. Normal syntax is designed for a
> law-abiding reality, for a reality that is organized temporally,
> spatially, and causally. In dreams these laws are suspended,
> too. And images in dreams can represent two things at once,
> as when we dream of X and know all the time that it is Y.
> This is why punning is the language of the night.

There is a nighttime reality, ruled by the moon and stars, so
different from daytime experience, dominated by the sun and greater
clarity. Dreams, of course, inhabit the night, though they also appear
in modified capacity as fantasies during the day. I believe the night is
more of a female realm. The yin/yang symbol suggests that the dark
yin portion is associated with female energy. So, too, do we connect
the moon and its many phases with women. Joyce was able to draw
on this nighttime world in his work, not just in *Finnegans Wake* but
also in *Ulysses*. To compose from that perspective forces the writer
to give up the usual syntax and order, to allow the night's erratic
energies to rule. It's a stunning realization for me given that I haven't
quite trusted the poems I've created that take this more experimental

approach—experimental in the sense that they don't follow the mainstream grammatical structure or usual ways of lineation in a poem. Here's an example:

CODA
A woman ages   preserved by light
not touched by strange

All she wants is a ride but
no one speaks
her language (no lessons or side
trips)
Through rear-view
rising and falling headlights
drop off
She swerves
cursing time
the car

Of course, I don't mean to imply that what we might call day poetry (poems that follow a traditional narrative and are conventionally punctuated and lineated) doesn't have value or only represents a masculine-yang perspective because it's more associated with the sun. That would be too simplistic. Yet in certain ways, I feel closest to what I'm here calling night poetry. It speaks as an animal might if an animal had language, meaning it has a preverbal quality, a sensitivity to its surroundings that the average human's eye/nose/ear can't access. When I read a poem I've written from that realm, it's often difficult even for me to understand what my unconscious is trying to say. But I get glimmers of meaning that make it worth the effort. As with "Coda."

In the opening line, there are two phrases. In the first, we learn that the poem is focusing on a woman who is aging and that she's preserved by light. I interpret light here to signify the day world that is dominated by sunlight, and there's something in that realm that acts as a preservative. It protects the woman from the night world as she's not touched by what's strange—whatever is unusual to our day consciousness.

The woman is seeking a ride. Perhaps she wants to flee aging itself but "no one speaks / her language," and there aren't any lessons or side trips that might help her out. Then through the rearview she sees "rising and falling headlights" that suggest something surfacing from the past, and then they "drop off." This artificial light has consequences and seems ominous, shaking her up so "she swerves / cursing time / the car." The poem suggests something circular going on, a pattern this woman can't seem to shake off.

Of course, the title, "Coda," has a clear meaning in that it refers to a concluding section, often of a musical event, but it also can refer to the last part of someone's life, as it does in this poem.

When I write in a more innovative mode, I want to surprise myself and my readers, shake us out of our usual expectations for a poem into—I hope—new ways of perceiving and feeling. I think "Coda" does this.

THIRTY-TWO

Earlier, I mentioned my interest in Henry Corbin's ideas. He continues to provide me with a provocative outlook on the world through the writings of Tom Cheetham, a Corbin scholar and a fellow of the Temenos Academy, an educational charity in London that offers education in philosophy and the arts from East and West sacred traditions. Cheetham has spent a couple of decades reading, ruminating on, and illuminating Corbin's texts—his theology—for lay readers like myself. I've just read M. Ali Lakhani's review of Tom Cheetham's *The Corbin Trilogy*, and the following lines that quote Cheetham within the review grabbed my attention:

> This dialogue of inner and outer, the Adamic language of "naming," is the Lost Speech we need to recover ... The loss of the imaginal dimension in modernity is evident in the loss of its primordial poetic sympathy, which Cheetham calls "that forgotten language and the energies that would return us home to a world we dimly recall." We can therefore define the urgent task of modernity as the need to recover the lost speech of the angels or the recovery of the poetic sensibility. The function of *poesis* is, in this regard, to unveil for us the reality of that personified and qualitative and sensate Presence through language that is both concrete and resonant of transcendence. Cheetham views poets therefore "as the guardians of the person and of the soul of the world," both inextricably linked so that "a violation of either is a violation of both."

When I read this review, and especially the emphasis it places on poetry's importance, I was reminded of a dream I had recently: I'd received access to a Jungian workplace. It was where analysts had their private offices and met patients, but there were also social areas and a library where members could congregate. I'd been given a tag to wear that identified me as a visitor and gave me access to the place. I recall there being lots of dark wood paneling and furniture that gave me a feeling of heavy, masculine authority. Some of the men I saw were handsome, and I wondered if I'd meet anyone who attracted me there. I did see my former female analyst at some point. She seemed to be engaged in an activity that would take her deeper psychologically. I also was meeting with a male analyst—no one I know in conscious life—who would be introducing me to whatever it was my former female analyst was doing that seemed to be connected to poetry writing, a kind of secret way to access the depths. At some point I was leaving this area and needed to descend on the elevator, but I was confused about which one to take. I eventually got it straightened out.

So here I am in this esoteric Jungian world, and I have access to all that's in there. Leaving that realm offers a challenge that I'm eventually able to figure out. In thinking about poetry giving access to places we ordinarily would not visit, it reminds me of when I write more experimental poetry. It seems to come from a different part of my interior, allowing that place in myself to speak to me and opening up an area I otherwise wouldn't connect to (and it could be tricky leaving such a place).

In recent years, I've tended to write more traditional lyric or narrative poems, and it's because M, who loves to read them, isn't as welcoming of the more innovative ones. After thinking about this dream, I feel a need to push back against my desire for his approval so I can access more often this different, experimental mode. So as wonderful as it is to share my work with him, I might be restricting myself by thinking of M as my only audience.

Much experimental poetry reinforces something I've intuited. When we let go of the grammatical structures that keep us under the control of an urge to rationality and let fresh configurations happen, we can sidestep the ego's control of such things and make contact with something more mysterious than what we access in daily life.

The dream seems to be offering a more expansive attitude toward writing poetry in that I have access to these Jungian offices and therefore to the ideas Jungians embody. The analysts working there seem attuned to the ways poetry, as well as dreams, can open us up to complexity and deepen us. This former female analyst may represent the dynamic feminine that I mentioned earlier who can think outside the box. In actuality, the woman represented here thought of herself as a maverick, and those of us who'd worked with her, both in the dream group I'd been part of for years as well as individually, celebrated that view of her, cheering her on. In the dream, she seems to be a part of myself that likes to step outside traditional modes of thought and feeling and may be responsible for what is stirring in me right now where I want to read and experience more about Hermetics and other mysteries.

Dr. Y said he thinks of me as someone who has both very conventional and very unconventional sides. Both are somewhat conscious, but both are there. My path to "wholeness" would be to integrate these disparate parts of myself so I'm not too one-sided.

What I'm taking away from this dream and my session with Dr. Y is that I need to read and write more poetry. I also must write more about its significance, its importance to me and others. It's dangerous that poetry is rarely read, at least in American culture. Consequently, we lose touch with something primal in our consciousness. I'm hoping that by reading Cheetham's books on Corbin, I'll become more aware of what that might be.

THIRTY-THREE

Since I'm still learning new things about myself and those I'm in relationship with, I'm excited to read Ram Dass's observation in *Still Here: Embracing Aging, Changing, and Dying.* He says, "the Soul is here to learn, and aging in all its inevitable difficulties is a prime learning opportunity." Dass confirms my belief that age is more than just an end game. It is the game, the time of life when we can truly honor our deepest natures and still make astonishing findings about ourselves.

This interior quest has been part of my daily routine for many years, not just as I've grown older, but I see it as more necessary when we age since it's the last opportunity to deepen our self-knowledge. As a writer, I've needed to nurture my inner life if I want to successfully create well-rounded characters or explore the multiple dimensions of the psyche through poetry and other arts. Writers have been our guides into the depths since the beginning of recorded time, and poetry itself can be one such guide into another realm. Wallace Stevens says, "What is his [the poet's] function? Certainly it is not to lead people out of the confusion in which they find themselves. Nor is it, I think, to comfort them while they follow their readers to and fro. I think that his function is to make his imagination become the light in the minds of others. His role, in short, is to help people live their lives."

Stevens not only was a poet, but as I've mentioned, he also was an executive at an insurance company, occupying the world of commerce and the world of art. Because of his dual nature, he understands humans who live double lives—outer and inner lives, though often the latter is nonexistent or neglected, as is true for many of us whose positions in the external world take precedence.

But poetry can be one way of stimulating our inner selves or helping us to make that inward journey. I see a parallel between poetry and dreams since I believe that both arise from a similar place in the psyche, the more archaic part of ourselves that isn't available to us except through images and symbols. The psyche seems preverbal, though this statement makes it sound as if it can't make use of language. A better way of putting it may be that the Psyche (with a capital "P")—what Carl Jung called the objective psyche or "collective unconscious"—has existed since the beginning of time, and our individual psyches hook into it. Dreams, poetry, and other art forms can communicate from this place, especially if they're transformative and capable of lifting us out of our ordinary perceptions.

For people who have no relationship with their dreams, they often seem arcane just as poetry does—nonsensical, strange. But once we become acquainted with how dreams engage with us, we discover that they speak a special language, not unlike the language of poetry; we need to read between the lines in order to hear the "message" that the dream contains.

But message sounds too much as if both poems and dreams are didactic, intentional creations. I don't start out writing a poem with a message. Rather, I have a feeling or image or idea I want to explore, or words just start flowing from my fingers onto the computer screen or through my pen. The poem is a place where I can make new connections between the world, memories, and language. Similarly, my dreams take the flotsam of daily life, mix it with memory, desire, and potential new life, creating a coherent, symbolic whole.

Yet to "get" a poem or a dream—"get" in the sense of developing a relationship with the contents, not necessarily understanding its meaning in a logical way—we need to enter it, walk around inside it, rather than examine it from the strong, sometimes harsh light of the rational intellect. Of course, we need to take our intellect with us—some aspect of it at least—but we descend into the dream or poem in order to "get it." In other words, to understand either a dream or a poem, we need to develop a new faculty—a "third eye or ear."

A number of years ago, I learned in a dream that poetry would provide the foundation for all of my writing, and I can see why that would be true. Poetry has not only been my favorite medium, but it also has opened me in ways that other genres can't. When I write fiction or non-fiction, I draw on a part of my brain that is happy with linear narrative, an arrangement of words that, for the most part, makes logical sense. Writing poetry has taught me to trust in the images that surface from the unconscious and not try to control them too much.

THIRTY-FOUR

WHEN MY HUSBAND WAS DIAGNOSED WITH BLADDER CANCER, our first response was shock and then "why him?" He had rarely even been ill with a cold and at eighty was in robust good health, his blood pressure consistently around 120/70 or lower. An avid in-door biker (an hour and a half each day, seven days a week) who follows a healthy Mediterranean diet, he seemed like the last candidate for this disease. But cancer has an omnivorous appetite, and unlike humans, it doesn't discriminate. It isn't selective in its targets.

As I wrote poems in response to what we were going through, I didn't consider publishing them because they were so personal. But when I reviewed what I'd done, I realized they needed readers because others will resonate with the emotions evoked. They aren't just diary entries to be hidden away. And while I don't like to publicize what my husband and I went through as a result of this diagnosis, I also realize my writing could be of value to others who are either experiencing something similar or who may do so one day.

Prolific Press also thought these poems needed an audience and published them as a chapbook entitled *No More Kings*. The first poem is entitled "Down the Rabbit Hole," and Alice's experiences in Wonderland aptly capture the disorientation we felt after receiving the cancer finding. It describes what I went through as I watched the urologist investigate my husband's bladder with a cystoscope. Since we non-medical types don't often get to see these cancers that grow in our bodies, I was fascinated at how innocent the growth looked. It, too, is part of nature, unaware of the havoc it produces in the lives it touches. And so, part of me, my writer self, was intrigued by this new world we'd entered.

Of course, a cancer diagnosis also reminds us of the inevitable prognosis we all face: everyone dies. Cancer just makes that reality more vivid. It becomes a new neighbor that we can't ignore, a dark cloud that hovers even during remission periods. We can never claim innocence again in terms of what lies ahead of us. The quotidian comes more into focus and takes on new meaning.

These poems capture some of the emotions I went through as I helped my husband encounter the many surgical procedures, chemotherapy sessions, and radiation appointments he tolerated. As I state in the poem "Bend in Seasons," "How super / natural the give and take / is between seasons, / as well as our mortality."

Please join me on the journey I've been on.

Down the Rabbit Hole

It looked innocent enough, this sea urchin
growing on my husband's bladder
floating in the sea
of his urine.

I watched it through the scope
a urologist had inserted into
my guy's urethra.

This uninvited visitor now resides
in his body, unaware
of the chaos
it is creating

or of me holding my husband's hand—wanting
to protect him. The surgeon
will scrape away the growth
and for a time we'll pretend

it never happened except
it did happen and now we know it can happen
to any of us and the world looks

less friendly from the inside of a scope
capturing images that stop

in time what in reality
can't be stopped.

A Bend in Seasons

September has crept
up on me, heavy
air a causality
of summer. Blossoms drop
their blooms, everything
in slow motion.

Even frogs feel the burden
—a bend in seasons
that skitters
across time. These letters
also sense a causality,
the way they mimic

dogs keening at the moon
and dump a lake
full of nouns without verbs
to prop them up. Something
fine wants to be
uttered. How super
natural the give and take
is between seasons,
as well as our mortality.

Word Game

On the surface
benign
seems so
benign
but for those
awaiting
a cancer

diagnosis
benign
looms
like cancer
itself waiting
to explode

Limbo

All my pockets are full
of dread
and I can't find
holes

to lose it
The sky is bright
blue

and the sun grabs
everything
in sight but it doesn't
change

what I feel
when my sweetheart
receives
another cancer diagnosis
It is night now
24 hours a day
and the sun can't break

through easily
and the end of the year
is approaching
and that makes me

sit up and take notice
but that's a cliché
so I can't use it here

I need fresh images

to convey what is resting
heavily on my heart

No More Kings

My husband wears a blue paper surgical hat
over his white curls and chats
with the nurse in the pre-op cell

at UCSF. His bladder cancer refuses
to leave and here I am waiting
with him for yet another resection.

It's too much to end
this year on a negative note.
I want good notes and not

this constant drumbeat of more
cancer and more surgeries.
I want him to breathe

easily and live so we can hold
each other at the end
and share our breaths knowing

there will be another one. It's too much
to think about this end game that sounds
like a card game and who gets the ace

or queen of spades. I want the queen
of hearts and diamonds and no more kings
because they want too much.

Loire Valley Love Song

At 9:23 PM, after
being overcast
all day, the sky
is mostly clear.
My beloved
clouds are back.
And so is the sun,
promising
a decent day
tomorrow.
I could live here,
nestled in all
this green
and forever
circling
the roundabouts,
refusing
to take
that final exit.

THE ESOTERIC

THIRTY-FIVE

IN MY THIRTIES, THE FIRST TIME I ATTEMPTED MEDITATION, I almost panicked. The leader had asked us to fix our half-shut, unfocused eyes on the floor for fifteen minutes and watch our breath exit our nostrils. He also said, "Don't attach yourselves to any thoughts entering your minds. Let them pass through, neither reacting to nor dialoguing with them."

It wasn't until I tried this simple meditation that I realized how dependent I was on my thoughts. I needed to identify with and be carried along by their flow, engaged in a constant inner chatter, just as some people keep on a radio or TV they aren't actually listening to for the white noise, needing to fill the empty spaces.

Of course, avoiding a dialogue with our inner selves has become easy with smart phones and all the other gadgets we can plug into, leaving no spaces for the aloneness that the theologian Paul Tillich discussed in a chapter on "Loneliness and Solitude" in *The Eternal Now.* In it, he makes penetrating observations about the plight of the modern person.

> Today, more intensely than in preceding periods, man is so lonely that he cannot bear solitude. And he tries desperately to become a part of the crowd. Everything in our world supports him. It is a symptom of our disease that teachers and parents and the managers of public communication do everything possible to deprive us of the external conditions for solitude, the simplest aids to privacy . . . an unceasing pressure attempts to destroy even our desire for solitude.

Tillich wrote this book long before the technological toys we currently possess existed. They make his observations even more prescient. Those of us who have spiritual yearnings, a desire to know the divine, however we may identify it, could be in serious trouble.

Tillich points out that God wants to "penetrate to the boundaries of our being, where the mystery of life appears, and it can only appear in moments of solitude." He concludes the chapter by daring the reader to risk knowing God by facing the eternal, and in the process to find ourselves, our true selves, not the false layers we wear as protection against God and our fellow human beings. Eknath Easwaran, a spiritual teacher and an author of meditation books, states that "Every major religion emphasizes this: to realize God, we must quiet the mind. As the Bible says, 'Be still and know that I am God.'"

To live with such awareness requires that we be awake, which isn't easy if we've spent most of our lives sleeping. It's not surprising that while we think we spend our "waking" hours in a conscious state, we are largely unconscious, using distractions to fill our time. The moment we get up in the morning, we jump on a treadmill of action that doesn't let up till we fall asleep at night. It's not an easy habit to break.

For those who find wisdom in the Bible, a passage in Mark that quotes Jesus warns us to "Be on guard! Be alert! You do not know when that time will come. It's like a man going away: He leaves his house and puts his servants in charge, each with their assigned task, and tells the one at the door to keep watch . . . you do not know when the owner of the house will come back—whether in the evening, or at midnight, or when the rooster crows, or at dawn. If he comes suddenly, do not let him find you sleeping." (Mark 13:33–36 NIV) The urgency of this passage impressed itself on me years ago when I was still a practicing Christian and attending a pre-Easter Bible study. I felt the words were addressing me directly, one of those rare epiphanies.

But I also recognized how difficult it was to be awake in the sense of this message. It means living as though your life depended on it instead of sleepwalking through your days. I didn't want to give up sleepwalking, yet I was curious about how I might wake up.

While I was regularly attending a Protestant church, I couldn't find methods within the institution to help me follow this Biblical urging. There were adult and children bible studies, but there were no opportunities to learn or practice meditation, even prayerful meditation, or any other spiritual discipline that would open the individual to the still, small voice within.

My quest to find opportunities to grow spiritually led me to an Episcopal retreat center in Inverness, California. Seekers were invited to stay there for formal or informal retreats. Food was provided as well as sleeping facilities. So, too, was a quiet environment where visitors observed silence during their entire stay. Surprisingly, the silence created an intimacy with others on a retreat that I hadn't expected.

Words can prevent us from communing on a deeper level than can happen through eye contact, body language, and touch—if we allow it. This "if" is a big precondition. There has to be some willingness to meet others and ourselves before it can happen. This realization led me to the mediation class I mentioned earlier and a quest for other ways of following Socrates's admonition, "know thyself." This included entering Jungian therapy and also paying closer attention to my nightly dreams.

My explorations also led me to Eastern religions, which tend to stress personal experience acquired through spiritual disciplines that can take the practitioners further inside themselves while transcending the limitations of the personality. Hinduism recognizes many paths to God that are chosen based on a person's personality. Huston Smith, in *The Religions of Man*, notes that the appropriate yoga practice is "a method of training designed to lead to integration or union," for "yoga comes from the same root as the English word yoke. Yoke carries a double connotation: to unite (yoke together) and to place under discipline or training (to being under the yoke, take my yoke upon you)."

Utmost in the yogi's training is the attempt to bring the senses and mind under control so that one's attention inward will not be filled with distraction. Smith continues, "'The senses turn outward,' observe the Upanishads. 'Man . . . looks toward what is outside, and sees not the inward being. Rare is the wise man who . . . shuts his eyes to outward things and so beholds the glory of the Atman within.'" The Bhagavad-Gita echoes this sentiment:

Only that yogi
whose joy is inward,
inward his peace,
and his vision inward
shall come to Brahman
and know Nirvana.

Another religion that stresses experience is Zen Buddhism. Concerned with getting the practitioner to see beyond the finger pointing at the moon to apprehending the moon itself, Zen masters insist on living experience. Smith points out, "Zen is not interested in theories about enlightenment; it wants to plunge its practitioners into enlightenment itself. The shouts, the buffets, the reprimands that figure in Zen training have nothing to do with ill-will. They are designed to help the student crash the word-barrier; to startle his mind out of conventional sluggishness into the heightened, more alert perception that will lead to enlightenment." Or to quote from the Bible, "Not everyone who says to me, 'Lord, Lord,' will enter the kingdom of heaven." (Matt. 7:21 NIV)

Just what is the nature of this kingdom, and why don't all professing Christians experience it? I believe there's a parallel between what Eastern religions call "enlightenment" and what some in the West call "the kingdom of heaven." One definition of enlightenment describes it as being "the uncovering of hitherto unknown powers of the mind." Similarly, the "kingdom of heaven" is within. It is a higher level inside each individual, higher than the ordinary earth-bound and sensual existence we are born into. Both enlightenment and the kingdom of heaven turn the focus from the external, temporal finite world toward the internal, eternal, and infinite realm.

The outer world represents all that is known and safe. There's the bank down at the corner where I deposit my money; the shopping center where I stock up on my material needs; the restaurant where I have physical and social hungers met; the bookstore where I can find out more about the visible and invisible world; the school that teaches me how to adapt myself to society; the friends who share my interests and values; and the church that confirms what I see in the world, offering me a community of believers who are as afraid as I am of the unknown, of the mysteries lurking within. Keep the noise level high so we won't have to hear the silence within.

Since fear seems to be the main obstacle to turning within, it's the first thing we must face if we want to live more consciously. If I had bolted during my first meditation session, I would still be running. Anxiety can be a great warning system to protect us from real threats, but it also can seize our lives, preventing us from taking the steps necessary to live as though our lives depended on it.

But fear also can be a great motivator, prompting us to challenge the many distractions that keep us from living less than a fully awake life, one where we try to hear those small voices within that want equal representation. Every day, I try to take those steps.

THIRTY-SIX

I LISTENED TO AN INTERVIEW TODAY WITH KAREN ARMSTRONG, a nun whose books about religion have opened many doors for me. She has published one entitled *Buddha*, and in the interview, she mentioned his admonition for people not to obey a doctrine that doesn't feel right or stand up to examination. We need to think critically, a principle that I believe in as well. However, my problem with Buddha is that he left his wife and son to pursue enlightenment—a spiritual ideal. To me, he's lacking something important if he looks for illumination mainly outside the home. Why isn't the home, the hearth, viewed as a source of enlightenment?

Follow a mother—or a stay-at-home father—day after day as she cares for her children and discover how much wisdom she gains from raising her kids as well as from the multiple tasks she engages in. Anyone—male or female—who has spent time raising children from infancy knows what gifts they can bring us. Observing how a human takes shape and the kinds of discoveries a child makes in life's zillion stages is one of the most profound experiences we can have, or the miracle of a toddler finding his or her vocal skills, first through gurgling and later by imitating his or her parents. Eventually, these indecipherable sounds begin to coalesce into words that at some point find their way into sentences. These sentences then lead the child into conversations with others as s/he finds how much impact s/he has on the world. It's always a miracle to witness the stages children go through from infancy to adulthood. And, of course, even after adulthood, our children continue to reveal themselves to us, just as we do to them. These changes continue until the day we die, especially if we're open to them.

Reading about Buddha giving up his material attachments makes me want to take the opposite direction, to go even more deeply into desire and connection, to praise the things of this world. I'm not attracted to austere, ascetic "spiritual" paths. I want all the mess of the world in my spirituality. I believe with Buddha that enlightenment or spiritual seeking should bring some joy. If it doesn't, to hell with it. Consequently, I don't want to blindly follow someone else's path. I want to find my own and trust that the Divine will guide me in that search. I want to take what feeds me from the various religions but not feel compelled to totally pursue their doctrines.

Maybe this urge resembles what I hope to find in a female approach to spirituality. Women must be able to move between multiple realities in a single day. If they have children, their care usually comes first. It includes all the elements that go into such care: introducing them to the world through reading to them; feeding them; playing with them; and making sure they have a safe, stable home life. In the process, they are the heart of the universe. Their blood pulses through their days as they keep us all connected to what's important in this life, as well as establishing human bonds—a major factor in the creation of responsive and responsible individuals.

I believe that over the centuries, we've been fed what I call more male approaches to spirituality and religion. They deny what it takes to not only live a good life but also to support the family. I want the more female approach that values nurturing and staying connected to the hearth, of living fully in the material world. This moment is all we know, so it's important to fully embrace it. But I'm also hoping there will be something beyond this earthly life when I die, and most religions share this perspective of life after death. Compassion also seems a major consideration in what I'm seeking in a spiritual path. If we can't walk in someone else's shoes, we're severely limited in understanding our own path, one of the reasons I'm so drawn to writing fiction and creating characters from totally different backgrounds than mine. I'm forced then to see things from multiple angles. And I like the idea of giving compassion a high place. But if I'm to honor my own standards, then I must feel compassion for the Buddha and others who take a similar route rather than being highhanded about my own views.

THIRTY-SEVEN

NO MATTER HOW MUCH I MAY DISCUSS AGING WITH DR. Y, I still have trouble embracing the reality that I'm old! In fact, many people don't live until eighty-one, and I could croak any day from some unexpected and unsuspected something lurking in this body of mine. Or I could fall and break a bone that will accelerate my road to the end. I'm living on borrowed time.

Because of that, I want to explore more fully the various esoteric traditions so I can enhance my understanding of the mysteries and what might await us beyond this life on earth, assuming there is a beyond, which I do believe. Somewhat. At least, I want to believe it, but in order to do so fully, I need more convincing data. I'm an empiricist at heart.

As I become more familiar with Henry Corbin and his ideas, I see that he also was a seeker, and he continues to interest me. So, I've ordered more of Tom Cheetham's books on Corbin, hoping to get a better grasp of his abstruse thoughts. But I'm also investigating other avenues, wanting to expand my horizons as I begin my descent into old old age.

Aha! I've admitted it. For the moment.

Recently, while I was reading an issue of the *Jung Journal*, an interview with a woman who has extensively researched the Tarot intrigued me, setting me off on that path as well, though I do question her inquiry and what has informed her position on this arcane practice. Tarot card users assume that they and their images can connect us with the past, present, and future. On the one hand, I love the idea that there is some ancient knowledge that we can plug into with the Tarot and other such mediums. But I'm also very skeptical of these side trips into the esoteric, even though Tarot, the I Ching, astrology, alchemy, parapsychology, and Hermetics all have something to say and attract me.

In the Jungian journal I referred to above, I also read a reference to Franz Bardon, a Czech occultist and teacher of Hermetics. After buying his book *Initiation into Hermetics* and starting to read it, I found much of the terminology obscure and the prose dense. I'm also put off by the hierarchical structure he paints in his descriptions of who has access to the rarified world he describes, but then, this is true of most of these explorers—their worlds have been shaped by a patriarchal view, and hierarchy is dominant in that mode. He says, "The more perfected, noble and purer a being is, he will therefore reside in a much purer and finer degree of density in the astral plane or sphere." This description is too reminiscent of the tiered aspect of life on earth, our need to climb the social and economic ladders if we want to be successful. There doesn't seem to be anything about egalitarianism or something beyond striving for higher or deeper levels of accomplishment.

However, the astral plane, or fourth dimension, is one of his concepts I've read about previously. He describes it as forming "the basis of everything which has an origin, regulation, and life existence, everything which has already occurred, is occurring presently, or will occur in the future in the material world." My very basic explorations of physics' string theory have given me another take on what Bardon calls the astral plane.

Some physicists think particles—matter in its smallest form—are made of vibrating strings. They're connected to eleven space-time dimensions. So the reality we're aware of in the four dimensions we occupy could be only a sliver compared to what actually is out there. Other worlds might exist near this one, making me realize how little we actually perceive just in terms of everyday reality. How limited we are! That's where many mystics come in as they appear to penetrate beyond the surface level of things, as I think certain artists do as well.

There also are physicists who believe time doesn't travel in a straight line. Our past could be still in the future or happening right now. Maybe our physical body can only exist in this one earthly element, preventing us from entering these other dimensions or even being aware of them. And maybe some part of us—our soul? our spirit?—lives on and travels to another level once it's free. We're a speck in the whole scheme, which limits our vision of what actually exists. Maybe death allows us to make the shift to one of these worlds.

Maybe this life is a preparation for something else, not just a dead end, a hole in the ground. Bardon claims, "that which is considered to be annihilation or death is merely a transition from one state into another." I don't know what gives him the authority to say this, but I do wonder if we shed this physical body at death and our spirit/soul shifts to the astral level. What about overcrowding? Who's in charge of population control there?

My next meeting with Dr. Y after reading some of this material came with the following dream: My husband and I had just moved into an enormous space. A younger version of my son L was part of this dream, and he seemed to have a brother as well, which isn't true in actual life. He was trying to help us unpack and had set up a table for four next to a window that overlooked a body of water. Since the place was so big, the table was farther from the kitchen than I was used to, and I worried about being so close to the water. We hadn't asked about the possibility of flooding before moving in. There also was a large fireplace and lots of wood for making fires.

But I hadn't been prepared for the crowds that poured into the place from 9:00 am on to take advantage of the vast amounts of free food that was set out on several tables. I learned later that a couple who also seemed to live in the place, or nearby, had committed themselves to providing free food on weekends. Fortunately, the crowds left after the food was gone, but this new space was becoming less and less appealing, especially because so much of the décor couldn't be replaced by our own things, and it was clearly not going to be our place alone. We also were next door to a church that attracted lots of traffic when it was open, even though the space we were renting was right on the edge of a town. This huge structure next to water started out so promising. But then the problems appeared.

I feel this dream is a response to the esoteric reading I've been doing. We've moved into this enlarged space that at first seems appealing. My young sons, who offer a fresh perspective, have much to contribute, including helping us settle into this place and making me aware of the water feature. At the moment it's a bonus, but it could flood in the future. So while being close to the waters of the unconscious might have benefits, it also could have a downside. Then we're overwhelmed by the crowds drawn to the house for free food, something we weren't aware of before we moved in. Could these people represent parts of myself that hunger for the kind of knowledge I'm seeking? This other dream couple has offered free food, and this is attracting these seekers, but their appearance seems dependent on the handouts they're getting and not on the food's quality.

Dr. Y wondered if I needed to find a balance between being open enough to let something new in but also having enough boundaries that I'm able to keep out more dangerous things. The dangerous things Dr. Y is referring to could relate to my initial reaction to some of the ideas in Bardon's book and how they're expressed, which also was true for a book on the Tarot that I purchased at the same time. In the dream, we were innocently living our lives when this huge space became available to us. This dynamic seems similar to how I anticipated reading these books dealing with arcane ideas and was eager to dive in, to feed on whatever spiritual nourishment I could find, to enlarge my living space. But after I started reading them, my response is similar to the crowds in the dream that dissolved once there was no more free food. There may not be the depth I'm seeking or true nourishment in these texts.

Dr. Y speculated that I might feel duped in a certain sense. What I thought I was getting is not, in fact, what I'm getting. I can be taken in by it, and it's not as if nothing is there because someone is providing free food for those who want it. There's nourishment, but it isn't clear how much value the nourishment actually has.

This meeting was extremely helpful. The dreams I shared, and the conversation with Dr. Y involving them, led to a discussion about Abrahamic religions and how they tend to be patriarchal and hierarchical, two approaches I have difficulty accepting. I want something fresh, something more neutral. He believes that I needn't be captivated by them but can find my own path, an idea that is both exciting and freeing. Exciting because I can be open to notions outside the mainstream, and freeing because I can trust in my own instincts and direction, something I haven't given enough credence to in the past. It's astonishing that finally, in my eighties, I can give myself permission to take this stance.

THIRTY-EIGHT

I'VE BECOME AWARE OF HOW THE *NEW YORKER*, THE *NEW YORK Review of Books*, and similar publications have invaded my precious reading period before I go to sleep. I spend enough time during the day inhabiting the world where these periodicals originate. But if I limit my nightly reading to them, I don't get to items that feed my spirit/soul. Last night, I tried to get back into Corbin's discussion of *mundus imaginalis*. The material is dense and complex but fascinating. It opens dimensions that expand my understanding of what might be outside of our everyday awareness. It also takes me into views more aligned with Eastern mysteries. I like being stretched in this way.

Reading Corbin's ideas is like looking at the heavens through a telescope, a mind-boggling experience I mentioned earlier that I had when my husband and I visited the Observatory B&B in Osoyoos, British Columbia, a few years ago. Since viewing the planets and stars visible via Jack Newton's incredible machine, I can no longer be content with the one-dimensional vista we have without it. The experience helped me to see how much more surrounds us in the universe than what our busy daytime lives—focused mainly on survival—cause us to miss. Our limited perception, overlain with our constant involvement with and inundation by various media, causes many of us to remain unaware of the incredible cosmos we inhabit.

A recent article in *The New York Times* by Farhad Manjoo, "Aliens Must Be Out There," underscores my belief that not only is there much more in the universe than we're aware of, but also that the blinders we habitually wear limit our ability to gain access to whatever might be out there. Manjoo quotes astrophysicist Avi Loeb, who tries to answer a question posed to him: if extraterrestrial life is so common, why haven't we seen it? Loeb, a professor at Harvard, argues that "the absence of evidence regarding life elsewhere is not evidence of its absence. What if the reason we haven't come across life beyond Earth is the same reason I can never find my keys when I'm in a hurry—not because they don't exist but because I did a slapdash job of looking for them?"

I'm grateful for scientists like Loeb who are making an effort to apply whatever resources they have to searching for what life may exist beyond our solar system. As Manjoo points out, "The sun is not special. I know that's a churlish thing to say about everyone's favorite celestial body, our planet's blazing engine and eternal clock, giver of light, life and spectacular Instagram backdrops. Awesome as it is, though, the sun is still a pretty ordinary star, one of an estimated one hundred to four hundred billion in the Milky Way galaxy alone. And the Milky Way is itself just one galaxy among hundreds of billions or perhaps trillions in the observable universe."

It's mind blowing to think that there are so many suns out there, suggesting that there could be other planets not unlike Earth or even more advanced than our planet.

Manjoo goes on to say, "Then there's Earth, a lovely place to raise a species but, as planets go, perhaps as unusual as a Starbucks in a strip mall. Billions of the Milky Way's stars could be orbited by planets with similarly ideal conditions to support life. Across all of space, there may be quintillions of potentially habitable planets, or even a sextillion—which is more than the estimated grains of sand on all of Earth's beaches."

Astonishing! Knowing of these possible worlds makes my interest in Corbin and other mystics' works more understandable. These seekers are motivated by a similar desire of many scientists who pursue knowledge beyond our everyday experience.

After finally making my way through Corbin's recital of what he means by *mundus imaginalis*, the different levels he perceives, and how they interact, I can see why he's so distressed by our everyday world's distortions of fantasy and image by grounding them in the mundane and missing the profundity of the Imagination with a capital "I." We've abused the idea of Imagination and its function, corrupting it in all the facile ways we corrupt images to sell products and elevate the destructive elements of our capitalistic system. We're part of this world that seduces us away from our transpersonal depths and keeps us bound by the bubbles we've created for ourselves. I fight this problem daily whenever I wake up for a few minutes and realize what I'm doing when I find myself immersed in 24/7 news or some other distraction.

It pleases me that Corbin, like Jung, doesn't try to become a guide for the individual seeker. They both believe each person is unique, and there are no rules we all should follow. Corbin insists we each seek our own guide, what he refers to as our angel, and that our paths in the end will be unique. What he offers is a great freedom, both a liberation and an anxiety-producing state. What if I don't find the right path or my inner guide? It's daunting to set off at my age on my own spiritual quest, almost as difficult as when I first left home at fifteen. Then I didn't have a clue about anything. It's amazing I've ended up so well.

Tom Cheetham has been an invaluable escort through Corbin's worldview. In *All the World an Icon: Henry Corbin and the Angelic Function of Beings*, Cheetham skillfully unpacks the main parameters of Corbin's thought. He also mentions Pavel Alexandrovich Florensky, a Russian Orthodox theologian, priest, philosopher, mathematician, physicist, electrical engineer, inventor, polymath, and neomartyr, who was killed by the Russian secret police in 1937. I'm drawn to Florensky because he supports my belief in dreams as being an important avenue to deeper knowledge. Cheetham says that Florensky thinks dreams give us access to imaginary space and time. Cheetham believes that Corbin would have approved of Florensky's view on dreams: "The dream world lies between the waking world and the invisible realm of the ideas, the spiritual world. The dream then moves between two worlds, and dreaming signifies movement between these worlds; it inhabits both worlds."

When I first read this, I resonated with the idea of dreams as mediators, but I suspect that, just as there are billions or trillions of galaxies beyond ours, there also are more than two worlds that dreams connect us to, making them an even more important tool for accessing the unknown. Cheetham comments on Florensky's thoughts on this movement by saying he goes "directly from the activity of the dream to the action of the artist. In the act of the Imagination that occurs in artistic creation we make this movement between realms." He then quotes Florensky directly: "In creating a work of art, the psyche or soul of the artist ascends from the earthly realm into the heavenly; there free of all images, the soul is fed in contemplation by the essences of the highest realm...then satiated with this knowledge, it descends again to the earthly realm. And precisely at the boundary between the two worlds, the soul's spiritual knowledge assumes the shapes of symbolic imagery. And it is these images that make the permanent work of art. Art is thus materialized dream."

I'm sure that neither Corbin nor Florensky believes that all artists are able to make these ascents and descents. And not all pour into their art the "essences of the highest realm." But those of us who are art lovers, whatever form it takes, can often tell when an artwork resonates at a deep level and awakens a similar response in us. As I've already stated, my houses of worship are museums, concert halls, theaters, books, and other entities where I can experience these messages from various worlds beyond our visible one.

THIRTY-NINE

I LOVE THIS QUOTE THAT I FOUND ON THE JUNG INSTITUTE website: "Our bodies and dreams may be our closest links to the unconscious, expressing the soul's longing through image, breath, gesture, the rhythm of our step, and the music of our speech. Dreams carry treasures that enhance the meaning and depth of our life's journey. Illuminating our inner landscape, they help us come to know disowned parts of ourselves, point to what we value, and provide guidance on our life path."

I'm continually astounded by the remnants thrown onto the shores of my conscious mind by the waters of the unconscious, those disowned parts of myself that insist on being recognized. I was thinking of the above quote when I met today with Dr. Y. I'd had an odd dream that I was eager to unload.

I'd dreamt that I'm part octopus. Someone told me I'd be taught how to live with this facet of myself. And that was the dream. I immediately wondered if the octopus was connected to the Corbin readings that have been preoccupying me. Could the person who is going to teach me how to live as part octopus be some combination of Corbin, Tom Cheetham, and even Dr. Y?

Not long ago, I watched a documentary, *My Octopus Teacher*, made by the diver and videographer Craig Foster who had spent a year forging a relationship with an octopus in a South African kelp forest. It was a moving testimony to the level of trust Foster created with this shy, wild creature, to the point where he was able to actually hold the octopus, and the creature responded to being stroked by the man. It also suggests that learning to live comfortably with my octopus self will take time and patience. We inhabit such different worlds that for each of us it could be a life-changing experience.

I was amazed to learn from the documentary I'd seen that each tentacle has its own brain, and octopuses are extremely good at hiding when they need to. But most are also sociable if the environment seems safe (an apt description of myself!). In order to conceal themselves from predators and for protection, many can change colors and hide inside whatever is available so as to avoid capture.

Given what I now know about these amazing underwater animals, it was very strange to awaken from a dream where I'd been told that I'm part octopus! Dr. Y's response to the dream was, "It's part of you. You are that, at least in part."

He also pointed out that the octopus is an image of multiplicity held together at the center. Each tentacle goes in different directions. Yet they're all unified through what's happening in its central nervous system. I reflected on all those tentacles that I may also have, and it reminded me of needing to take in Corbin and other mystics' material in multiple ways, not just through my intellect. I have to absorb it physically and emotionally as well. Otherwise, it's too complex. All of these tentacles can help me to access and understand the multiple worlds Corbin describes.

Of course, I've also been reading Cheetham's perspective on Corbin's views simultaneously, adding another dimension to what I'm taking in. One of the most important concepts for me is Corbin's belief that the imagination is not the imaginary. According to Cynthia Bourgeault: "Henry Corbin . . . introduced the term *Mundus Imaginalis* to name that intermediate, invisible realm that figures so prominently in mystical Islamic cosmology. But Corbin was drawing here on a highly technical and quintessentially Islamic notion of Imagination as being itself one of those higher and more subtle energies, possessing being, will, objectivity, and creative function."

She goes on to say: "To our modern Western ears, the word 'imaginal' may seem to suggest some private, interior, or subjective inner landscape, 'make-believe' or fanciful by nature. But while it is typically associated with the world of dreams, visions, and prophecy— i.e., more subtle forms—the imaginal is always understood within traditional metaphysics to be objectively real and in fact comprising 'an ontological reality entirely superior to that of mere possibility' (*Gospel of Mary Magdalene*, p. 153.). It designates a sphere that is not less real but *more real* than our so-called 'objective reality' and whose generative energy can (and does) change the course of events in this world. Small though it may appear to be, it is mighty, as those who try to swim against it will readily attest."

As Corbin himself said, Islamic theosophers referred to *Mundus Imaginalis* as the "eighth climate." And it's the imaginative consciousness, the cognitive imagination, that perceives that realm. As Florensky has noted, some artists work from this visionary level, and it helps me to understand how some people become so engrossed in works like Rothko's paintings that have no perceptible image in them but convey something extraordinary. I've experienced a similar response at times when in museums. I'm thinking of Jackson Pollock's work. I could sit for hours in front of his drip paintings, completely transfixed. The artwork is communicating with us from other dimensions whether the artist realizes it or not.

Given that Corbin, like Jung, doesn't try to guide individual seekers, I feel liberated. He's giving me permission to find my own way, just as Dr. Y has suggested I do. It's not so much me finding a spiritual leader who will show me the way, but that I can follow my own path. I've thought that I don't have any special ability to enter these realms. And even though my dreams are helpful in some ways and give glimpses of something more than our everyday reality, I denigrate my own capacity for seeing more deeply into the heart of things.

But now that I have an octopus as part of my makeup, maybe I have access to its multi-layered, multifaceted abilities, where each tentacle has its own brain, its own intelligence. It's also at home underwater with knowledge of that medium that I don't have, perhaps signaling I could experience a closer relationship to the unconscious given that water is often associated with our depths. So now I need to ask: what is my path?

Dr. Y thinks the way I answer that question and try to explore it will reveal what is true for me. He believes my writing, reading, teaching, and relationships are all included in my path. It's what I do and how I live. Though I might not be able to follow Corbin and others' ways to explore what's beyond, it doesn't mean that my approach isn't valuable or valid. Dr. Y also observed that my reading about Corbin is helping me to not only think about who I am but also how I am. And the octopus dream speaks to an image of what it is to be me. Multifaceted? Multibrained?

When I discussed with Dr. Y my explorations into Corbin and others, he commented that I seem drawn to the esoteric traditions and the promise they make of another realm. Since I mentioned my resistance to the arcane language I'm running across in some of these texts, he suggested that I pay more attention to my own writing and thinking. He believes I may discover that I have a lot of inner wisdom if I listen the right way.

I'm afraid I don't see myself as a wise woman and insisted I don't know anything. But he said these other published seekers don't either. He pointed out that they come from certain learned traditions and are speaking from what those traditions teach. He contrasted them with people who have experience in the world and speak from their personal knowledge, sharing what they've learned. I'm assuming he puts me in the latter group. He believes that 95 percent of these so-called "guides," self-proclaimed experts and mystics, are making fraudulent claims.

Of course, lots of people like myself get caught up in their ideas, if that's what they are, rather than trusting what Dr. Y calls the "path of not knowing." He thinks if we don't know, then sometimes we discover something new. He claims I'm the only person who can help myself in terms of transcending everyday life if I pay attention to whatever is happening. But I have to not know in order to find something new. Dr. Y believes that some exceptional people—Buddha, Jesus, Mohamad, Moses, for example—made discoveries and were gifted at conveying what they learned to others. But he thinks we have to not know in order for something new to emerge. The esoteric works I'm reading can sometimes point a way, but they can only communicate something that I, Lily, might aspire to. But I still have to walk my own path in my own life and fall into my own holes.

Still, though I'm not a practicing Christian, one of the most profound things I take away from my days of reading the New Testament is that there is another plane, or other planes, or other dimensions. Jesus was seen after death, and others also have been reported as having been seen after death. So parts of the New Testament offer a window into mysteries that we have no answer for at the moment. Does it demonstrate that there is an afterlife? Worlds within worlds?

At this point in my life, since turning eighty, I want something to counter the many views about death as the final curtain. And I want knowledge that pushes back on an otherwise ominous end. I bought these books in the hope that they would expand my vision of myself and the universe I inhabit so I can face the end with less fear and loathing. When I told Dr. Y I was going to continue diving into these texts investigating esoteric material to see what I can discover, his response surprised me. He believes the most important thing to me, psychologically speaking, is not necessarily what these texts have to say but the interest they've awakened in me. All of which is me—the reactions I have to reading these works. He thinks what happens inside me when I'm drawn to this material is authentic—deeply. That's where the transformative wisdom is.

His comments made me recall that I spent twenty celibate years after I divorced my second husband. I lived alone during that time and read many books by and about mystics, including a study of William Blake's writings and his amazing images. I also regularly meditated and did yoga. Both practices played a major role in helping me to become more centered and created the foundation for who I am today.

At the end of our session today, Dr. Y said that if I take the octopus seriously, I'll have a very different view of who I am from now on. Not just who I am but what I am—part human woman and part multiarmed, multibrained octopus.

ASCENT

FORTY

A SCENT IS THE WORD I'M USING TO END THIS EXPLORATION of the ways I've sought meaning from dreams and the arts. I'm assuming the descent that started me on this narrative should end in an ascent. In psychological terms, the descent and ascent motif is a metaphor for ego-consciousness contacting the unconscious. Through my work with Dr. Y and in writing this book, I've made a descent. But now that I'm nearing the end of this particular journey, it's time to ascend, though I do hope it isn't a foreshadowing of the final ascent that might actually be a descent!

Living through the COVID-19 pandemic has forced me to pull back from the outer world and live within much narrower circumstances. I've been unable to attend concerts, plays, or movies; socialize with family and friends; visit restaurants; or travel. In a way, this period has mimicked how the very old must restrict their movements because of physical or mental impairments.

While I could have done without the accelerated rehearsal, this past year has demonstrated that M and I can live culturally rich lives under constrained circumstances. Though we haven't attended concerts at Davies Hall featuring our wonderful San Francisco symphony, we have subscribed to the Berlin Philharmonic digital concert hall and have had access to an amazing array of concerts highlighting the greatest conductors, composers, and musicians from around the world. Its archives offer an ongoing feast for the music lover. Thanks to the Internet, we've also visited major museums— St. Petersburg's Hermitage, Ft. Worth's Kimbell, Houston's Menil collection, the Louvre, the British Museum, and so many more. As for food, while we've missed dining at fine restaurants, we've continued our Saturday date night by ordering a variety of take-out offerings from the East Bay and Marin County that have more than satisfied us. To create an elegant experience for ourselves, we often use tablecloths and candles, the food served with good wine that we've had delivered. We also have an incredible music accompaniment, one of our favorites being Michael Tilson Thomas's *Keeping Score* series on several major composers that is now available on YouTube.

I'm sure others have made these discoveries as well, setting the stage for when our forays beyond our immediate living space will be minimal—mainly to doctors and dentists. But we can still live an abundant cultural life via the Internet. Of course, M and I are both great readers of print and audio books, so the worlds they encompass stimulate our imaginations and deepen our understanding of ourselves and others.

And my dreams continue to offer unexpected insights into myself. In one of my recent dreams, I was involved with a man who was in charge of a Jung Institute and seemed tuned into me and my needs. I guess he'd had this administrative role for a long time. I was touched when he gave me a large, delicately frosted, pastel blue bowl accompanied by a bunch of rocks and something else I can't recall. I rearranged the items so the rocks were inside the bowl, rather than separate from it. This change made the bowl and other objects much easier for me to carry. To counter my fears of aging and losing M, as well as a world that seems to be fragmenting, falling into pieces, along comes this inner male who offers me a symbol of something that can hold the parts together and keep the collection intact.

It appears as if all the rocks that are now contained inside the bowl might represent individual entities that are currently connected because they're inside this glass container. Dr. Y wondered if the bowl's round shape and ability to hold all these disparate things wasn't an image of the self. The bowl holds all the potential oppositions and contains them almost like a symbolic expression of the self. He also wondered if something I need right now is an image of wholeness as I become more aware of my unconscious thoughts and the role they play in my life.

I told him that I've been intrigued by Corbin's ideas about angels, specifically, that we each have one from birth. I felt that there was a strong parallel between Corbin's ideas about angels and Jung's take on the Self. I've wondered where my Angel is and how I can contact him or her? I'd actually asked myself that question, and a few nights earlier, I'd dreamt that I was making contact with a powerful figure, and that was the whole dream. Is this powerful figure my Angel? Will s/he be revealed more fully as time goes by? I don't know. But it seemed related to the blue bowl dream, except in this one, the Angel seems to be manifest.

This experience led me to a discussion by Roberts Avens from "Henry Corbin's Teaching on Angels." He says,

> Each earthly being has his Fravarti, a heavenly archetype or angel . . . While the soul of a being and its double are one, they are separated upon entry into a body. The one, the heavenly twin or pneuma, remains in heaven, while the other enters a body. The lot of the fallen soul is to search for its other half, the original heavenly twin . . . Expressed philosophically, the soul is from the organic body a completely independent substance. The body serves only as a temporary dwelling place. The soul's "true, real body," its angel, is a heavenly body of "pure immaterial matter" or a "raiment of Light" that it will dress itself in again at the end . . . Every creature consists of an earthly component and a heavenly counterpart, its archetype or angel.

Dr. Y pointed out that the angel is a messenger between the divine and the human. In Greek and Hebrew, it means messenger. In Jacob's Ladder, a bridge between heaven and earth, there are angels traveling from above to below, as well as from below to above. We send angels to the transpersonal, and we receive angels from that level. If we're living totally unaware of these other beings and states, then we don't have much to send above, so to speak, but according to Corbin and the Sufi mystics he writes about, if you're really awake to the Imaginal, to the reality of the Imaginal (or as Jung calls it, the reality of the psyche), the ego also has messages to send and to receive from above. Of course, it goes totally against the reductive materialism of our modern culture and sounds like two crazy people talking via Doxy.me!

I agreed. Even just taking dreams seriously can be suspect. Most people don't think of dreams as being anything serious.

But I take them seriously and so does Dr. Y. That lead me to tell him about another dream that seemed related to the blue bowl. I was attending an event that included several women I seemed to know in the dream world and maybe in the external world as well. There was going to be a ball on all four nights of this event, and the women really got into preparing for it. All were wearing ball gowns with extremely full skirts that would have been popular in the 1800s or earlier. Every one of them was stunning, colorful, and buoyant. But I had worn something much simpler. I realized I needed to smarten up before the next ball. I knew that M would enjoy seeing and dancing with all of these lovely women, though I worried he might like it too much!

My first thought after telling Dr. Y about this dream was that the costumes' shapes, the skirt at least, resembled inverted bowls. And all of these women were celebrating these dresses that had gone out of fashion. They emphasized something wonderfully feminine, though maybe an idealized female image. Still, however much we might criticize such outfits from the ego's external world perspective, in the unconscious, they are something to rejoice in. Wearing them made something magical happen to the women. They stepped out of the ordinary world (they couldn't just walk down a street in today's cities without looking out of place), but they needed the special container of the balls in order to wear them freely. So, in a way, these balls were containers for the dresses just as the bowl I received in another dream is a container for the rocks that accompanied it. The same process, the container and the contained, is happening. And it gives me an image of disparate elements merging to reflect on.

Dr. Y felt I was touching on important material in these dreams that might help me through hard times.

FORTY-ONE

Seeing myself on Zoom during this pandemic has been like looking in the mirror while wearing my contact lenses: chilling. Age lines that I can ignore when looking in a mirror without wearing corrective lenses cut into my face. The skin on my neck resembles the texture of prunes. My hair grows grayer every day, white threads turning my previous dark brown color into a muddy version that doesn't quite know what it wants to be, and I have solid white patches framing my face. Clearly, I'm not going to leave this world "gracefully." If anything, I'll go out with a big thump.

But I am enjoying teaching my current Fromm memoir workshop. The students, most of them near my age, are bright, thoughtful, fun, and adventurous. They love having an opportunity to engage with each other in small groups on Zoom via the breakout rooms. They exchange drafts of the current assignment and give each other thoughtful feedback on how to improve the narratives they're writing. Eager to dive into other people's life experiences, they're helping to validate them. What a gift they are to each other and to me! I always learn as much if not more from these older students than they do from me. For a short time, the class creates a community of individuals who fully appreciate the hive we build together that produces something sweet and lasting.

I also appreciate their stories and their willingness to dip into past moments and write about them. Many of their narratives are instructive in how to practice ego integrity versus despair, our last psychological stage of life that Erik Erikson described. He believed most people pass through eight psychological stages. In the last, we need to hold on to our sense of wholeness while avoiding despair—the fear that there is too little time to begin a new life course. It also is a time when we can contemplate our accomplishments and develop a feeling of inner integrity if we see ourselves as having led a successful life.

When my Fromm students write about their past, they are reclaiming parts of themselves and also discovering the ways in which they have led fulfilling lives. While no one can avoid feeling despair at times, even before reaching old age, it's easier to manage it if we still feel absorbed in the world and with others. Writing our memoirs gives us an opportunity for such engagement. And the act of writing offers a chance to revisit previous experiences as well as the opportunity to reflect on them—to discover meaning in what we may have previously overlooked.

Teaching these classes has made me want to dip into my early years as well, and I have ample resources for doing that—the journals I kept from my late twenties on. While five years of these daily musings were destroyed in my Harcourt Street fire, I still have many that survived. Recently, I've been carving time out of most days to return to those times in my life and to read my journals' contents.

When I first tried to keep a record of what was happening in my life, I started by recording my dreams on note cards. I have a big bundle of those that survived the fire—covered with cramped writing, their edges blackened. I later graduated to lined notebooks. Then, in art stores, I discovered hardcover volumes of plain white paper that suited me better. I didn't have to write within the prescribed ruled lines and could include sketches from dreams or other areas. The paper was stronger, and the journals themselves felt more permanent, as if I were making a deeper commitment not only to my dreams and other ruminations but also to myself, to the discovery of a self through their pages.

In the process, I found a ballpoint pen that had four colors: red, green, blue, and black. I loved being able to categorize what I was writing by using these colors: green for dreams; red for enlarging on the dream images and themes, as well as recording meetings I had with a Jungian analyst I worked with then; blue for reflections; and black for recording important moments from my days that I didn't want to lose.

I recently came across the following passage that I wrote in November of 1976:

> More and more I want these writings to be purely private, records for myself to refer to as the drama of my life unfolds,

rather than public utterings; writings to be kept within my immediate family, or else completely destroyed. These personal dialogues with myself are too precious to be shared outside of my closest circle of family and friends.

Rereading them now, I'm amazed at how rich my dream life was then. The journals include pages of green, the pasture from which my nightly theater arose. I still find the dreams fascinating to read as in many I'm working out relationships with others and discovering parts of myself I hadn't known existed. But most important, I think, was my belief that airing the dreams in my journals gave their images a place to reside. I also felt that whether I understood them or not, they had an impact on me, even though I may not consciously know what their effect might be.

I also made a discovery in a journal from 1976, after I'd taken a class with M, the man who became my husband in 1994 and is the love of my life. I was reflecting on what would be the best place for me to attend graduate school, and I wrote, "I think a major part of what draws me back to SF State is the futile hope that M and I will meet and become 'lovers.' More than lovers really. I do want marriage." This remark was after I'd had several dreams in which I was experiencing a growing relationship with this former teacher, at that time, someone I'd only had a few words with during class. But he'd had a tremendous impact on me intellectually, and I experienced a deep awakening that semester. It's amazing that we did meet and end up marrying almost twenty years later. Did I dream our relationship into existence?

In reading Henri Corbin's ideas on the role of imagination and Tom Cheetham's elaboration on Corbin's thoughts, I realize I'd stumbled on something important that I'm now fully recognizing. As Cheetham points out in *After Prophecy*:

Corbin's life-work is a prolonged and profound meditation on the power of the image in the service of the individual. A primary means by which imagination becomes embodied is language—through poetry and story...It is the great challenge of human existence to find an entry into that stream of life—to find the myth we are living.

As Cheetham and Corbin insist, "We are imagining animals. We live and die by the imagination." *In Dreaming Myself into Old Age*, I've tried to show some of the ways dreams and the arts are vitally important to humans in cultivating our imaginations, the faculty that not only can help us to create, but also to become more conscious of something profound stirring in our lives, the source of the mysteries we encounter.

During my search for others who are writing about the end days, I came across *Old Age* by Jungian analyst Helen Luke. I was particularly drawn to her comment that aging is a mystery. It *is* a mystery. Since so many elderly people tend to exit the mainstream world where they've worked or raised kids or pursued a career or calling, it's no wonder that this penultimate journey remains invisible to many who don't yet inhabit the senior universe. Hence, it's largely unknown. But it's also a mystery in the sense that our stage of life happens immediately before death claims us. So the finiteness of death makes these last years seem more difficult to penetrate, to understand. What exactly is it that we're doing other than trying to hold ourselves together until we can no longer do so? Is there another purpose to our final years?

Erikson believed that if we see our lives as unproductive, are guilty about our past, or feel that we did not accomplish our life goals, we become dissatisfied with life and can develop the despair that leads to depression and hopelessness. But success in this stage can lead to the virtue of wisdom. Sagacity enables us to look back on our life with a sense of closure and completeness, and also to accept death without fear.

I hope Erikson is right and I can reach that kind of tolerance of my mortality. I long for such a state to take me over! According to this website on Erickson, "Wise people are not characterized by a continuous state of ego integrity, but they experience both ego integrity and despair. Thus, late life is characterized by both integrity and despair as alternating states that need to be balanced."

I believe much of our despair in old age involves the physical decline of these wonderful bodies that have carried us through so many life stages, something I've rarely mentioned in these pages and have not wanted to think about too much. Yet it can't be denied. For some people, minor ailments as well as chronic conditions can accumulate and be overwhelming: arthritis; diminished hearing and seeing; problems with bladder control; sleep difficulties; and the threat of dementia shutting down our thinking and memories, the structure from which we construct a self. It's difficult to sustain a high level of self-esteem if we feel as if we're falling apart.

But I have more concerns. After going through a few weeks recently when my dreams became sparse and seemed to partially dry up, I also worried that I was losing my lifelong companions that have accompanied me this far on my journey. It would be devastating to lose them now. I mentioned my fears to Dr. Y and wondered if memory loss was the cause.

He suggested that instead of judging the process, "Try to observe the change that is happening at this moment. What does it mean? Be curious about why your dreams are different now than when you were younger. Try to suspend the judgment and be impartial toward yourself. When you have a judgement about a part of yourself, it forecloses whatever might be there that's unfamiliar."

His comments made me realize that by judging what was happening, I was somewhat responsible for shutting down my dreams. Since admitting to that possibility, I seem to have freed them to continue visiting me in the night.

But I'm still left with the question: Who am I, then, within this diminished house I'm walking around in? One aspect of aging's mystery is the new identity many of us must create for ourselves out of the fragments we're left with. It's like making a collage from the remaining workable aspects of our beings. And that requires that we first acknowledge what's going on and use our imaginations as the glue to hold our older selves together.

In Thomas Moore's introduction to Helen Luke's *Old Age*, he points out that Luke sees the Fool as an apt archetype for the aged.

> Her models of aging are eccentrics and fools—holy fools, of course: Odysseus, Lear, and Prospero. I take it that the best way to move into old age is to allow the fool to come forward, to become more and not less an individual following mad attractions . . . She is talking about the art of release, the surrender of self, and the paradoxical discovery about what has always been present but never fully embraced . . . As Helen Luke intimates, aging is a matter of imagination.

I don't know what Moore means by imagination, but it has been a central theme in my quest for knowledge, informed by mystics and other artists, a well that we all can dip into for refreshment and invigoration. When I lose this capacity to imagine other worlds or other passages, then I also lose something important about myself. I become static rather than dynamic and stop the life force from invigorating me. I hope I don't reach that point. If I do, I hope my imagination will not be squelched entirely but will help me resume what for me is the essence of life, my ability to see beyond the immediate moment and enter the unknown.

The image of the Fool in many Tarot decks depicts a young man approaching a cliff's edge, but he's seemingly unaware of what awaits him if he continues moving forward. What more apt description of our final days on this earth! We all are faced with this challenge of not knowing what will happen after we've stepped off into the abyss. We can have our hopes and dreams, but, ultimately, we are all Fools, taking off into the unknown. I'm hoping that I can take these steps with the same fervor I've always had in approaching a new adventure.

EPILOGUE

ON DECEMBER 16, 2022, STEVE JOSEPH, MD, KNOWN IN these pages as Dr. Y, died. His death was unexpected. My last meeting with him was on November 16, 2022. He had planned to take off Thanksgiving week as well as the week following that holiday. Our next appointment would have been on December 7. But I received a call from one of his colleagues on December 6. He told me that Steve was undergoing a continuing medical problem and wouldn't be able to see me the following day when we had planned to resume our Zoom meetings, necessitated by the pandemic. I never saw him again.

Death often is startling and sudden, startling because it's so foreign, no matter how many losses we may have experienced in our lives. And sudden because it follows its own timetable, one that may not match ours.

Two years younger than I am, Steve tried to help me view our end days as a natural process. I had entered this late life analysis because of my fears of aging and death, so it was a factor that we periodically addressed. In July 2022, during one of our weekly sessions, I had mentioned to him that, because of our age, it finally was becoming more real to me and M that we are near death. We're both in our eighties, M three years older than I am, a time when our bodies begin to show more wear. No matter how young I may still feel, I'm eighty-two, and my body is beginning to register that age, even though my mind still resists the idea.

Though M and I love to fantasize about taking trips, with COVID and other concerns, our major travels may be over. At times, this stage feels like being in limbo waiting for the "main event." Now I find myself thinking more about what might await me when death arrives. How will I meet it? What do I expect? What can I reasonably expect? How can my mystic leanings give me something substantial to carry me through? It seems so desperate, but I do at times feel desperate the more I think about what we're facing. I'm afraid it's going to get harder to act as if we'll live forever and still enjoy each day thoroughly under these circumstances. What else can I do to better prepare for the end game?

In one of our recent sessions, Steve had said Jung believed that in the unconscious, death is not the end. Rather, it's a symbol of a transformation where an older thing deintegrates so something new can be born. Steve felt Jung's take on what Kafka believed was the meaning of life (death) was symbolically true, even though we just come to an end physically. In the inner world, there may not be a dead end. Yet there may be a transformative end where something old gives way to something new. Death and rebirth, death and resurrection: all the world's wisdom teachings are about that understanding.

Then he mentioned he'd had a chance to read my article "Dreaming Myself into Old Age: One Woman's Search for Meaning" that the San Francisco Jung Journal had recently published. It compresses a few of the things I present in this book-length version.

He said, "I got the journal and read your article. First, I like it a lot and think it's really a great accounting, but it also helped me to understand the role our work is playing in your process. I understand more deeply what it means to you and what it carries for you. I'm very appreciative and glad that I'm helping you in that way. But I don't think of myself as an old-testament patriarch!" As I've mentioned earlier in these pages, at our first meeting, I had thought he resembled an old-testament patriarch.

I said that I believed he has some of those qualities.

He said, "Okay, maybe I have a little bit of that, and Dr. Y is an interesting choice of letters."

I said, "You may not recall, but when I first started working on Dreaming Myself into Old Age, I asked which you'd prefer to be called, Dr. X, Dr. Y, or Dr. Z. You said Dr. Y."

"Dr. why not?"

"Exactly!"

Then he observed, "It's been a long time, hasn't it. A lot of work for you. We've known each other a long time already."

And I responded, "I don't know what my life would have been

like if I hadn't had this opportunity weekly to make this descent into my final years with you. It's enriched my life tremendously."

That was the end of the session. I thanked him, and he said, "You're welcome. We'll talk again in a week."

Steve gracefully and wisely shared my dreaming and awake moments. I'm sorry for many things about his untimely death, including not being able to attend a public memorial. But I especially regret him not reading this book that features him, though mainly in the background. Given my experience of Steve over the years, I feel the background would have been his preferred place. One of his responses when we were talking about dreams or other matters that will stay with me is "I don't know." It takes a lot of courage and authenticity for an analyst to admit that he isn't all powerful and all knowing. His response gave me and my psyche space to be the knowers.

With Steve gone, I now face a new phase as I enter 2023. I have no idea what it will bring. Change requires transformation, loss, and inevitably grief. Now, I'm facing all these things along with the uncertainties that a new year presents. Yet I do have this memoir as a constant reminder of the richness I've experienced not only in my younger life but also in this time when Steve was a most helpful guide.

ENDNOTES

1. https://frithluton.com/articles/self
2. "The Red Wheelbarrow" by William Carlos Williams was originally published without a title and was designated as "XXII" as the twenty-second work in Williams's book *Spring and All* (Contact Publishing Co., 1923).
3. Marianne Moore, "Poetry," in *Others for 1919: An Anthology of the New Verse*, ed. Alfred Kreymborg (Nicholas L. Brown, 1920).
4. Bonnie Costello, *Marianne Moore, Imaginary Possessions* (Harvard University Press, 1981). All quotations by Costello in this section come from this book.
5. Marianne Moore, "An Octopus," *Observations* (Dial Press, 1924).
6. Marianne Moore, "The Monkey Puzzler," [title later changed to "The Monkey Puzzle"] *The Dial* (January 1925).
7. https://en.wikipedia.org/wiki/Hetaira
8. Rebecca Futo Kennedy, "Elite Citizen Women and the Origins of the Hetaira in Classical Athens," *Helios* (Spring 2015).
9. Susan E. Schwartz, "Puella's Shadow," *International Journal of Jungian Studies* (September 2009).
10. Google's English dictionary provided by Oxford Languages
11. Encyclopedia Mythica, https://pantheon.org
12. Nicholas Kristoff, "What's So Scary about Smart Girls?" *The New York Times* (May 11, 2014).
13. Christopher Vasillopulos, "Through a Glass Darkly," *Jung Journal* (Winter 2014).
14. Ann Belford Ulanov, "Aging: On the Way to One's End," in *Ministry with the Aging: Designs, Challenges, Foundations,* ed. William M. Clements (Routledge, 1989).
15. Florida Scott-Maxwell, "The Measure of My Days," in *Revelations: Diaries of Women*, eds. Mary Jane Moffat and Charlotte Painter (Vintage Books Edition, 1975).
16. https://www.rt.com/usa/202255-many-interacting-worlds-quantum-mechanics
17. William Stafford, *Writing the Australian Crawl* (The University of Michigan Press, 1978).
18. George Orwell, "Politics and the English Language," *Horizon* (April 1946).
19. Rainer Crone and Joseph Leo Koerner, *Legends of the Sign* (Columbia University Press, 1991).

20 Wilner, Eleanor, "The Closeness of Distance, or Narcissus as Seen by the Lake," *The Writer's Chronicle* (December 1998).

21. Bernstein, Charles, "Semblance," in *Postmodern American Poetry*, ed. Paul Hoover (New York: W. W. Norton & Company, 1994).

ABOUT THE AUTHOR

 In her youth, LILY IONA MACKENZIE, a poet and novelist who also writes nonfiction, frolicked on a Canadian farm in an area almost too small to be on the map. She didn't practice writing then, but she did learn to pay attention to her surroundings. The clouds in the sky offered images that stirred her imagination and stimulated her dreaming self. Cows, calves, sheep, pigs, chickens, turkeys, dogs, cats, and horses were her early teachers and her main playmates. Those years instilled in her the need to honor those in her care and the realization that being successful involves hard work. As a writer, it includes her dedication to the writing craft and her belief that commitment and perseverance form the machinery that writers depend upon.

SHANTI ARTS

NATURE ▪ ART ▪ SPIRIT

Please visit us online
to browse our entire book catalog,
including poetry collections and fiction,
books on travel, nature, healing, art,
photography, and more.

Also take a look at our highly regarded art
and literary journal, *Still Point Arts Quarterly*,
which may be downloaded for free.

www.shantiarts.com

Printed in the USA
CPSIA information can be obtained
at www.ICGtesting.com
LVHW011137180923
758424LV00007B/144